GLOSSARY OF VITAL TERMS
FOR THE HOME GARDENER

Robert E. Gough, PhD

SOME ADVANCE REVIEWS

"The most complete glossary of home gardening I have seen. The definitions are concise and easy-to-understand. This excellent reference book should be on the bookshelf of every avid gardener."

Richard J. Shaw, PhD
Associate Professor, Plant Sciences
University of Rhode Island

"Will certainly become a permanent fixture in my personal library as well as in the reference section here. . . . Students and volunteers will now be able to quickly find definitions of technical gardening terms in simple language. The glossary is organized in easy-to-follow alphabetical fashion and includes everything from grafting and layering to confusing taxonomy terms that can discourage even the most ambitious gardener."

Kathleen M. Mallon, Director
Cooperative Education Center, Greenhouse Conservatory
University of Rhode Island

"A valuable addition to the beginning gardener's library as well as a quick, easy guide for the more experienced gardener who wants a straightforward explanation of terminology. An important contribution."

Harrison G. Hughes, PhD
Horticulture Professor
Colorado State University

NOTES FOR PROFESSIONAL LIBRARIANS AND LIBRARY USERS

CONSERVATION AND PRESERVATION NOTES

Glossary of Vital Terms for the Home Gardener

FOOD PRODUCTS PRESS
An Imprint of The Haworth Press, Inc.
Robert E. Gough, PhD, Senior Editor

New, Recent, and Forthcoming Titles:

The Highbush Blueberry and Its Management by Robert E. Gough

Glossary of Vital Terms for the Home Gardener by Robert E. Gough

Seed Quality: Basic Mechanisms and Agricultural Implications edited by Amarjit S. Basra

Statistical Methods for Food and Agriculture edited by Filmore E. Bender, Larry W. Douglass, and Amihud Kramer

World Food and You by Nan Unklesbay

Introduction to the General Principles of Aquaculture by Hans Ackefors, Jay V. Huner, and Mark Konikoff

Managing the Potato Production System by Bill B. Dean

Marketing Livestock and Meat by William Lesser

The World Apple Market by A. Desmond O'Rourke

Understanding the Japanese Food and Agrimarket: A Multifaceted Opportunity edited by A. Desmond O'Rourke

Marketing Beef in Japan by William A. Kerr et al.

Glossary of Vital Terms for the Home Gardener

Robert E. Gough, PhD

Food Products Press
An Imprint of The Haworth Press, Inc.
New York • London • Norwood (Australia)

Published by

Food Products Press, an imprint of The Haworth Press, Inc., 10 Alice Street, Binghamton, NY 13904-1580

Library of Congress Cataloging-in-Publication Data

Gough, Robert E. (Robert Edward)
    Glossary of vital terms for the home gardener / Robert E. Gough.
      p. cm.
    ISBN 1-56022-036-8 (acid-free paper).
    1. Gardening–Terminology. 2. Gardening–Dictionaries.
I. Title
SB450.95.G68   1993
635'.014–dc20   92-45029
                                                                CIP

To My Wife,
Pat

ABOUT THE AUTHOR

Robert E. Gough, PhD, is the former President of the Northeast Region of the American Society for Horticultural Science and a leading specialist in small fruit and viticulture. His experiences as a county agricultural agent, state and regional extension specialist in small fruit, professor, and senior research scientist have provided him with a great deal of insight into the needs of growers.

Introduction

George Gordon, Lord Byron, once remarked that nothing was so difficult as starting a story except, perhaps, ending one. Beginning this book was quite easy, actually. There were hundreds of terms bouncing around in my brain at any given time, but determining how many of those to put down was difficult. I have tried to include those terms that home gardeners are likely to encounter and for which they may not already know the definition. In browsing through European works you might come across the term "bourse." This is as uncommon to the modern American gardener as the old American term "scandigie." But you must know each to make sense of the text and the practices described. As modern gardening feels the heavy influence of science more and more, new pest-resistant cultivars are being introduced, each with its own important abbreviation–"N," "F," "VFN," "RN." The inquisitive, well-educated gardener is curious about plant growth, and botanical terms such as "stele," "phototropism," and "phyllotaxy" become important for understanding the complex nature of plants. New technology has coined common terms such as "decorticated," "pelletized seeds," and "mil," all of which frequently appear in today's seed catalogues. Additionally, there is a contemporary counter-movement away from modern scientific gardening, back to the commendable practices of "double-digging" and "frost-seeding." Whether a practice is old or new, European or American, scientific or traditional, it carries its own vocabulary. Sometimes, gardening is tough enough; to stumble over the terminology is a shame.

In this book I have tried to include all the terms the home gardener will likely encounter. The number in parentheses following most entries identifies the reference work from which the entry was adapted. I have supplied the definitions for entries having no number. Necessarily, hundreds of terms have been omitted. Plant names, except for general terms such as "everlastings," have been excluded, as have most specific diseases and insects. General diseases, such as "yellows" and "rust" and animal pests such as "mites" and "thrips" have been included because they are commonly a source of trouble. You are not likely to encounter a discussion of the "endoplasmic reticulum" in a monthly gardening magazine, and the term does not appear here. But you might encounter "cuticle" and "epidermis" and therefore they are included.

This book is a glossary, not an encyclopedia. It is meant to be a handy pocket guide for the home gardener, not an exhaustive reference work for the scholar. Terms are defined but not fully discussed. To do so would require a multivolume work that would be quite expensive and most inconvenient.

To enjoy anything, you must understand the language. Gardening is no exception. But the less time spent poring over a reference work cluttered with minutia, the more time is left to enjoy the garden. When you come across an unfamiliar term, look it up here. Then, go enjoy your plants.

R. E. Gough
Oakfield, Maine

A

A: (A1). In tomatoes, the disease resistance code for Alternaria (early) blight.

abscission: Defoliation or the dropping of a leaf, fruit, or flower. (9)

abscission zone: A layer, or layers, of cells where specialized cell division leads to the separation of a plant part. (4)

acaulescent: Plants or plant parts that are essentially stemless, such as dandelion. (11)

accent plant: A plant with a well-defined decorative effect used in the landscape to enhance a particular design feature. (10)

accessory bud: A lateral bud formed at the base of a terminal bud or at the side of an axillary bud. (19)

accessory fruit: Fruit having some parts derived from tissue other than that of the ovary, i.e., floral tube, receptacle, etc. (4)

acclimation: (acclimatization). Adaptation to light, temperature, etc. (4)

achene: A dry, one-celled, indehiscent simple fruit, such as the "seeds" of strawberry and sunflower. (4,14)

acid-forming: Term given to fertilizer or other material that leaves an acid residue in or on the soil. The strength of the acidity is expressed as the amount of pure limestone (calcium carbonate) required to neutralize the residue. This number is called the "equivalent acidity." The equivalent acidity per ton for some common materials is given below.

   ammonium sulfate: 2,960 pounds calcium carbonate
   ammonium nitrate: 1,200 pounds calcium carbonate
   cottonseed meal: 200 pounds calcium carbonate
   urea: 1,500 pounds calcium carbonate

Other materials that leave an acid residue are ammonia, ammonium phosphate, dried blood, castor pomace, diammonium phosphate, fish scrap, guano, sewage sludge, process tankage and urea-formaldehyde. (1,2)

acid soil: Soil having an acid reaction, that is, a pH below seven. (1,3)

acre: A unit of square measure equal to 43,560 square feet, or an area of 208 feet square.

acre-foot: The volume of water or soil covering one acre to the depth of one foot. It is equal to 43,560 cubic feet or 27,000 gallons.

acropetal: Produced in the direction of the apex. (19)

actinomorphic flower: A flower with radial symmetry.

acuminate: (attenuate). Leaves that taper to a long, thin point. (11)

acute: Sharp-pointed. (11)

additive: (amendment). A substance, such as sawdust, compost, etc., added to the soil to improve friability, alter pH, etc.

adjuvant: A material added to a spray to increase the action of the main ingredient. (9)

adnate: Unlike structures closely fused to form a single structure. (11)

adventitious: Plant organs appearing in an unusual position or at an unusual time. (4)

adventive: A plant that has been introduced but not yet naturalized. (15)

aedicule: A recess or niche in a garden wall for placement of a statue.

aeration, soil: The process by which atmospheric air replaces soil air. Air in poorly aerated soils contains more carbon dioxide and less oxygen than air in the atmosphere. (3)

aerial bulb: See bulbil.

aerial root: A root formed on aboveground portions of the plant, such as in epiphytes or some ivies. (10)

aerobic: Having oxygen as part of the environment. (3)

afterripening: The maturation of a seed after harvest and during its dormancy. (9)

aggregate: A unit of soil structure usually less than ten millimeters in diameter. (3)

aggregate fruit: Fruit from a flower having many pistils all ripening together, as in raspberry. (4)

aggregation: The process which binds primary soil particles (sand, silt, and clay) together, usually through biological activity. (3)

agricultural lime: See lime.

agriculture: The science of farming. (18)

agstone: Agricultural limestone. (2)

A horizon: The surface layer of a mineral soil. It has the greatest amount of biological activity. (14)

air-dry: Drying to the point of equilibrium with moisture in the air. (14)

air-layering: Propagation of woody plants wherein the roots form at a point of intentional wounding along the stem, which is then separated to produce the second plant. (11)

air plants: See epiphyte.

al: See A.

albino: A plant or portion of a plant lacking chlorophyll. (14)

alkaline-forming: A fertilizer or other material that leaves an alkaline, or basic, residue in or on the soil. The strength of the alkalinity is expressed by the amount of calcium carbonate equivalent and termed "equivalent basicity." The equivalent basicity per ton for some common materials is given below.

bone meal (steamed): 500 pounds calcium carbonate
nitrate of potash: 460 pounds calcium carbonate
nitrate of soda: 583 pounds calcium carbonate

Other alkaline-forming materials include basic slag, borax, calcium nitrate, cocoa shell meal, dolomite, magnesia, dried manure, oyster shells, peanut hull meal, some peat, phosphate rock, animal and garbage tankage, tobacco stems, and tung meal. (1,2)

alkaline soil: A soil having an alkaline, or basic reaction, that is, a pH above seven. (1)

alkali soil: (sodic soil). A soil that has a quantity of available sodium large enough to interfere with crop growth. It may also have large quantities of other soluble salts.

allee: Old spelling for alley. A narrow passageway in a garden, usually framed by trees or shrubs. A common feature of Italian Renaissance and sixteenth century French gardens. (8,10)

allelopathy: The condition wherein one plant excretes a compound or compounds that are toxic to another plant. (17)

alluvial: Pertaining to processes or materials transported or deposited by water. (3)

alpine: The region between the timber line and permanent snow line on mountains. (8)

ALS: In cucumbers, the disease resistance code for angular leaf spot.

alternate bearing: (biennial bearing). The tendency of a cultivar to bear a heavy fruit crop one year (called the "on-year") and a light crop, or no crop, the following year (called the "off-year").

alternate host: Some plant diseases, such as the rusts, require two different plants or hosts to complete their life cycle. Such plants are termed "alternate hosts."(18)

aluminum sulfate: A material formerly used to acidify the soil for plants such as rhododendron, azalea, and blueberry. It has little nutritional value and its misuse can cause toxic aluminum buildup in the soil. (2)

amendment: See additive.

ament: See catkin.

ammonia: A gas made up of 82.25% nitrogen and 17.75% hydrogen, by weight. It can be used as a fertilizer or in the manufacture of nitric acid and urea. (2)

ammonification: The formation of ammonia or ammonium compounds. (1)

ammonium nitrate: A synthetic material made by oxidizing ammonia to nitric acid and then neutralizing the solution with gaseous ammonia. This material contains half its nitrogen in the ammonia form and half in the nitrate form. Commercial fertilizer grades contain about 33% nitrogen. (1)

ammonium phosphates: The two important compounds used as fertilizers are monoammonium phosphate (11-48-0) made by combining phosphoric acid and ammonium, and diammonium phosphate (21-53-0, 18-46-0, and 16-48-0) made by combining ammonia with monoammonium phosphate in solution. (1)

ammonium sulfate: (sulfate of ammonia). Nitrogen fertilizer (21-0-0) containing all its nitrogen in the ammonium form. It is also a source of sulfur and is valuable for acidifying the soil. (1,2)

amoena: An iris with white or very light-colored standards and deeply-colored falls. (12)

An: In melons and cucumbers, the disease resistance code for anthracnose. A number following indicates the race of the pathogen.

anaerobic: Absence of molecular oxygen. Anaerobic environments are usually detrimental to higher plants over time. (3)

analysis: This word, applied to fertilizer, designates the percentage composition of the product. The first number gives the percentage nitrogen, the second number the percentage phosphorus, and the third number the percentage potassium (potash). These are separated by hyphens, as in 5-10-10. A fourth number, usually referring to boron or magnesium, sometimes appears but must be explained on the label. (1,2)

analysis plan: A rough drawing of an area that will be landscaped. It indicates future construction features as well as topographical and environmental data.

anchor root: See brace root.

andromonoecious: A plant producing many male flowers for each female flower. (17)

angiosperm: A group of seed-bearing plants possessing enclosed ovaries and flowers. (14)

angle of repose: The angle formed with the horizontal of a slope at equilibrium. Used when referring to a pile of loose material such as fertilizer, sand, and mulch. (2)

anion: A negatively charged ion, such as Cl^- and $SO4^{--}$. (3)

annual: A plant completing its life cycle of growth, flowering, seed production, and death in a single year. (8,14)

annual ring: The secondary xylem added to a woody stem each year. (14)

anther: The male, pollen-bearing sac situated near the top of the filament. One of two floral parts making up the stamen. (4)

antheridium: The male sex organ in plants of groups other than angiosperms and gymnosperms.

anthesis: The time of bloom and pollen release. (4,10)

anthocyanin: Blue, purple, and red plant pigment. (4)

antrorse: Directed forward or upward. (16)

apetalous: Without petals. (11)

apex: The tip of a shoot or root containing the apical meristem.

apical dominance: The influence of the terminal bud in suppressing growth of lateral buds. (4)

apical meristem: Meristematic cells near the tip of a root or shoot which give rise to all cells of the mature tissue. (4)

apiculate: Having a small, pointed tip. (16)

apogon: An iris having no beard. (12)

apomixis: Plant reproduction in the ovaries without fertilization. (9)

apothecium: A fungal spore-producing structure. *pl.* apothecia. (4)

appressed: Lying against an organ. (16)

approach graft: The procedure wherein two independent plants are grafted together. The young plants are bent together and grafted with an inlay, tongue, or splice procedure. Each remains on its own roots until the graft is healed.

aquatic: (water plant.) In horticulture, any plant that grows submerged, floating, or on the border of ponds and lakes, including marsh and bog plants. (10)

arbor: An open structure with horizontal framework, supported by columns, upon which vines or other plants are trained. The structure is subordinate to the plants. (8,10)

arboreal: Pertaining to trees, or living in trees. (8)

arboretum: A collection of woody plants grown for educational and scientific purposes. (18)

arboriculture: The growing of trees for shade or ornamental purposes. (8)

arborist: An expert in the art of arboriculture. (8)

arch: A framework similar to an arbor but acting as the primary feature, with the plants secondary in importance. (10)

archegonium: The female sex organ in plants other than angiosperms.

arcure: A tree trained to a trellis in a series of arches. (13)

are: A metric unit of area. One are equals 1,076.40 square feet. (8)

aril: A fleshy ring around the seeds of certain irises and some other plants. (12)

aristate: Awned. (16)

arm: In general, any tree branch. In grapes, the term refers to a branch more than a year old. (10)

artificial manure: See compost.

As: In tomatoes, the disease resistance code for *Alternaria* stem canker.

asexual: Vegetative, as in asexual propagation. (4)

ashlar: A rectangular block of dressed stone. A masonry wall of such stone. (8)

attenuate: See acuminate.

auricle: The earlike lobes at the base of grass blades. (16)

auriculate: Having auricles, or ear-shaped appendages at or near the base of a petal or leaf. (15)

auxin: A group of naturally-occurring and synthetic plant hormones that primarily stimulate cell elongation, but also promote root formation. (4)

available: Forms of a nutrient able to be taken up by the plant. They are usually soluble in water or certain ammonium compounds that might be found in the root environment. When applied to water, the term refers to the water that can be absorbed by the plant, lying between field capacity and the permanent wilting point. (1,2,3)

awn: A stiff, hairlike structure found in the inflorescence of certain grasses, such as oats and barley. (10)

axil: The angle between the shoot and a leaf petiole, branch, etc. (4)

axis: The main line or stem. (10)

B

back-bulb: An old false- or pseudo-bulb of an orchid. (10)

background planting: Taller annuals or perennials planted behind the smaller annuals of a bed. A hedge, tree, or group of trees that supply a suitable background for a garden or building. (11)

bactericide: A chemical used to kill bacteria. (19)

bagasse: The dried residue of sugarcane left after juice extraction, used as an additive to growing media and similar to peat moss. (14)

balled and burlapped: (B&B). A plant dug with a ball of earth which is wrapped with burlap to protect the roots.

banding: Placement of fertilizers close to the seed at planting or, sometimes, along the plant row before or after emergence. See also side dressing. (3)

bare-rooted: Plants dug and the soil shaken from the roots.

bark: The outermost woody, mostly dead portion of the trunks of trees and shrubs, the main function of which is to protect the vital tissue beneath. (10)

bark bound: An unusual condition wherein the wood of a tree expands faster than the bark, causing the latter to split and crack. (11)

bark graft: The type of graft wherein several scions are inserted beneath the bark of the stub. A knife is used to make several two-inch-long cuts through the bark, which is gently peeled back and the butts of the scions inserted. The bark is then folded back over the scion butts and tacked or taped in place.

bark inversion: The practice of removing a ring of bark and reinserting it upside down on a tree trunk to dwarf the tree.

basal plate: Stubby, fleshy shoot axis in a bulb.

basal rot: A disease, caused by a fungus, that rots the basal plate and sometimes the bulb in narcissus, crocus, hyacinth, and freesia. (11)

basic slag: A by-product of steel manufacturing from phosphatic iron ores. It contains about 12% total phosphoric acid, not less than 80% of which is soluble in 2% citric acid. It also contains about 46% calcium oxide, 7% magnesium oxide, 4% manganese oxide and 14% iron oxides. Phosphate slag not conforming to this definition is designated low grade. (1,2)

basin: The slight depression in the blossom end of fruit such as pear and apple. (10)

basipetal: Proceeding toward the base of an organ. (19)

bast: The phloem.

bay: A physical division of a greenhouse. (5)

bayonet hoe: An implement with a narrow, trowel-like blade used for weeding and thinning young plants. (11)

BB or B&B: Abbreviation for balled and burlapped.

beard: A stiff, hairlike awn, often in tufts. A fringe of tissue, as in iris and some orchids. (10)

bed: An area of ground where flowers or potted plants are grown. (5)

bedding: In tillage, the mounding of soil into elevated beds. In animal husbandry, the organic material spread on the barn floor to absorb excrement. (3)

bedding plant: An herbaceous plant used in the landscape or in planters and flower boxes, most frequently an annual, but sometimes a perennial used as an annual. (9)

bedrock: The solid rock underlying soils. (3)

beet hoe: A small, hand-held implement with one or two points and a sharp blade used for thinning and weeding beets and other small seedlings. (10)

belvedere: An open garden shelter located upon a hill commanding a view of the surrounding countryside, usually made of brick or masonry. (11)

bench: A raised, built-up area, usually in a greenhouse, where flowers or potted plants are grown. The word may also be used as a verb meaning to transfer plants from outdoors to pots on a bench. (5,10)

berry: A simple fruit with single or multiple carpels having a fleshy pericarp with no accessory parts (a true berry) or with accessory parts (a false berry). The term is also commonly but incorrectly used in referring to any small fleshy fruit. (4,10)

B horizon: The layer of soil beneath the A horizon. It often contains some humus, silicate clays, and metal oxides. (14)

biennial: A plant normally completing its life cycle in two years. The first year is characterized by vegetative growth; the second by flowering, fruiting, and death. (8)

biennial bearing: See alternate bearing.

bifid: Having two clefts. (15)

bilabiate: Having two lips, as the flowers of *Salvia.* (15)

binding plant: A plant such as creeping willow, black locust, and others with rhizomes or stolons which help to hold soil against erosion. (11)

binomial: The two scientific names indicating a genus and species, such as *Daucus carota* (carrot). (14)

biocide: A combination fungicide/bactericide used to preserve cut flowers or as a sterilant. (14)

biodegradable: Capable of being decomposed by biological processes. (3)

biodynamic gardening: A system of plant and soil management originated in Europe by Dr. Rudolf Steiner. This system encompasses the concept that the garden is a biological unit wherein all elements and operations are interrelated. (11)

biological control: Using natural forces, such as predators, to control harmful pests. (11)

biomass: Total mass of living organisms in a given amount of soil or other environment. (3)

biostimulant: Organic, growth regulator-like material that stimulates the growth of plants. (9)

bipinnate: Having two sets of pinnae. (15)

bitone: An iris with standards and falls of different shades of the same color. (12)

biuret: A product formed during the manufacture of urea that is toxic to plants. (3)

bizarres: (bizard). In carnations, a flower striped with two or three colors. (11)

black frost: The damage occurring to plants when the temperature drops below freezing but remains above the dew point. There is no hoarfrost, and the only indication of the low temperatures is the blackened plants or plant parts; hence the name.

blackheart: The killing of cells in the wood of apple trees because of a single midwinter cold spell. (9)

black knot: Long, black growths on the shoots of stone fruit, particularly cherry and plum, caused by a fungus. (15)

black leg: A disease of geraniums, cole crops, and potatoes causing the stem to blacken and die at the soil line. (10,15)

black rot: A disease of cabbage, apples, and certain other plants, causing black spots and decay.

black spot: A fungal disease causing black spots, yellowing, and defoliation in rose, delphinium, and elm. (11,15)

blade: The flattened portion of a leaf.

blanch: (ridge). An operation that reduces the amount of chlorophyll in a stem, such as in celery and asparagus, by banking soil about the stems or by covering them with paper or boards to exclude the light. Cauliflower is traditionally blanched by tying the outer, wrapper leaves about the head. (10)

blast: The sudden death of young plant parts, such as flowers and fruit. It may be caused by pathogens or by environmental adversities such as frost. (11)

bleeding: (weeping). The harmless exudation of sap from a wound. (11)

blend: An iris in which the color yellow and another color are intermingled. (12)

blight: A general term to describe the withered or decayed condition of plants. (8,10)

blind: The failure of a plant to produce flowers and/or fruit. (10)

blind bud: A bud that is stopped in development and is shed or remains latent and rudimentary. (13)

blind shoot: (blind wood). A shoot that does not terminate with flowers; applied especially to roses. (5,6)

blindstoken: Killing the flower before planting to increase the weight of tulip bulbs. (9)

block garden: A type of vegetable garden wherein plants are grown in groups rather than rows. (19)

blood: A by-product of the slaughter industry containing quickly available nitrogen. Blood has about 13% nitrogen, 1.5% phosphorus, and 85% organic matter. (2)

bloom: Flowering. Also, the thin powdery waxy substance on the surface of some fruit, notably blueberries, grapes, and plums. (4)

blossom-end rot: The breakdown near the blossom-end of fruit such as tomato, usually caused by imbalances in soil moisture and/or calcium.

blotch: A disease symptom appearing as a dark mark or irregular pattern on a fruit or leaf. (11)

bluestain: The blueish stain on lumber or wood, especially pine, caused by several fungi species. (11)

bluestone: See copper sulfate.

blue vitriol: See copper sulfate.

bog garden: A garden cultivated in low, wet ground using plants suitable for such locations. (11)

bole: The unbranched trunk of a tree. (9)

bolt: To go to seed, usually in the sense of premature flowering. (17)

bone meal: Raw meal is composed of cooked and dried animal bones finely ground. The fineness of the grind governs the availability of its nutrients. Raw meal contains about 4% nitrogen, 23% phosphorus, and 31% calcium. Steamed meal is made from grinding bones previously steamed under pressure. It contains about 2% nitrogen, 27% phosphorus, and 35% calcium. (1,2)

bonsai: The art of growing small trees in containers. The size of the plant is maintained through top pruning, root pruning, wiring, and other methods. (18)

borax: A chemical compound containing about 11% boron. (1)

bordeaux mixture: A very old fungicide of varying formula. One common preparation is 4-4-50, meaning four pounds of copper sulfate, four pounds of hydrated lime, and 50 gallons of water. (11)

bordeaux paint: A paint made from bordeaux mixture by the addition of enough linseed oil to make a paste. (11)

border: A long bed of flowers edging a walk or lawn. (18)

boron: A minor element essential for plant growth. (1)

botany: The science of plants, their characteristics, functions, and life cycles. (14)

botrytis: A fungus that causes numerous diseases such as blossom blights of zinnia and marigold, gray mold of geranium and primrose, and several storage rots of fruit. (11)

bottom heat: Heat supplied by placing heating cables or steam pipes near the bottom of a bench or bed.

Bouche-Thomas: A training system for fruit trees employing a minimum of cutting and mostly bending and weaving of the young branches.

bough: A main branch of a tree. (13)

bouquet: An arrangement of cut flowers or other plant parts without a container. (11)

bourgeon: A developing shoot.

bourse: The thickened base of the cluster of apple and pear. (9,13)

bower: A simple summer garden shelter. (11)

brace graft: A type of graft used to provide a natural brace in young trees. A pencil-thick shoot from one side of a weak crotch and about 12 inches above the crotch base, is wrapped around an adjacent branch on the opposite side of the crotch. About six inches of bark is removed from that branch to the precise width and pattern of the wrapped shoot. The bottom tissue of the young shoot is removed and the shoot fitted into the incised area, then tacked in place. The tip of the shoot is trimmed to a wedge shape and fitted beneath the bark of the branch.

brace root: (anchor root). An adventitious root arising from the stem of some plants for support of that plant, as in corn. (14)

bract: A modified, usually small leaf just below the flower on certain plants. Some bracts are showy, such as the red bracts of the poinsettia and the pink or white bracts of the flowering dogwood. (4,5)

brake: A place overgrown with brush. A thicket. A name loosely applied to any coarse fern, but referring specifically to the genus *Pteris*. Sometimes used synonymously with the term "bracken."(8,11)

bramble: A shrub or vine of the genus *Rubus*. It usually refers to raspberry or blackberry, but more broadly, to any thorny or prickly woody plant. (4)

bramble hook: (cane cutter, pruning hook). A long-handled cutting hook with a curved blade used to reach the crowns of raspberry and blackberry canes for pruning.

breaker: A device attached to a water hose to reduce the force of water without reducing the volume. (6)

breaking: Opening, sometimes prematurely, of the flower and/or leaf buds, either in spring or after pinching. (10,11) (Of tulips): The separation of colors into irregular streaks or stripes. Variegation. (11)

breastwood: Shoots that grow outward from an espaliered tree. (13)

breezeway: (dogtrot in southern U.S.). A roofed, open way between two buildings, as between a house and an attached garage. (8)

bridge graft: A type of repair grafting wherein scions are inserted into sound tissue below and above a wound, thus spanning the injured area and providing healthy tissue for the transport of water and nutrients.

brindle: (brindille). A thin, lateral shoot usually ending in a flower bud. (13)

broadcast: The scattering of seed, fertilizer, or other substances over the soil surface without regard to rows or drills. (3,11)

broad-leaved evergreen: Outdoor plants having broad, evergreen leaves, that are not conifers. The group includes holly, rhododendron, mountain laurel, andromeda, etc. (10)

brown heart: The browning and breakdown of the center of the root caused by a deficiency of boron in turnips and rutabaga.

browning: A condition of evergreens wherein the foliage becomes a rust color. It may be natural or indicate some degree of damage from a variety of causes. (11)

brown rot: A fungal disease that attacks stone fruit. (11)

brushing: The use of brush to construct a temporary windbreak or to otherwise modify a plant's environment to speed growth. (14)

brutting: Breaking the terminal of a young shoot in the summer and leaving it partially attached to the branch. (13)

buckhorn: (dehorn). To heavily cut back the main branches of a tree to remove damaged wood or to prepare for topworking. (9)

bud: An undeveloped shoot with leaf parts (leaf bud) and/or flower parts (flower bud) protected by scales. (4)

budding: A form of grafting using a dormant vegetative bud instead of a scion for insertion into the stock. Production of a shoot from an underground plant part. (4)

bud scale: A modified, scale-like leaf that protects the bud from winter drying. (4)

bud sport: See sport.

bud stick: A shoot, usually one year old and dormant, from which buds are removed in budding operations.

bud union: (graft union). The point of attachment of the scion and the stock upon which it has been budded or grafted.

buffer capacity: The ability of soil to resist a change in its pH when acid or alkaline materials are added. (1,2)

bulb: A globe-shaped, modified underground stem that has a terminal bud surrounded by fleshy modified storage leaves, as an onion and tulip. (5)

bulbil: (aerial bulb, brood bulb) A rounded mass of cells formed on the stems of certain plants at the axils of leaves. When detached and placed in the proper environment, they will develop into a new plant. Essentially, a bulb borne above ground. (8,10)

bulblet: A small bulb usually formed near the base of an older, larger bulb. (9)

bulb-pan: A shallow pan for forcing bulbs. (9)

bulk density: The mass or weight of a known volume of soil. (14)

bullhead: A malformed rose flower wherein the center petals are short and the flower blunt. (6)

bullnose: A physiological disorder in narcissus that results in the failure of the flower to open after the gooseneck stage. (9)

bundle scar: The location on a leaf scar where the vascular bundles have detached. (19)

burr: A spiny covering on a fruit, such as on chestnuts. Also, any plant bearing such spiny fruit. (10)

burl: (knaur). A large knot growing on the trunks of trees. (10)

burned lime: See calcium oxide and lime.

burning: A condition of various causes, such as intense heat and cold, excessive wind and fertilizers, all of which result in rapid dehydration of plant tissue and subsequent cell death. (11)

burr knot: A stem swelling containing root initials commonly found on quince and apple. (9)

buttress root: An enlarged root, extending above ground, that gives support to tree trunks.

C

caespitose: Matted. (15)

calcareous soil: Soil having a pH greater than seven due to the presence of free calcium carbonate. This soil will effervesce visibly when treated with hydrochloric acid. (1)

calcium carbonate: The main ingredient in limestone, oyster shell, and marble. (2)

calcium chloride: A calcium salt sometimes applied to dirt roads or paths to reduce dust and to melt ice. It is also used in solution to fill rear tractor tires for increased traction. (8)

calcium nitrate: A white salt formed by reacting limestone with nitric acid. It contains about 17% nitrogen and 34% calcium. (1,2)

calcium oxide: (lime, burned lime, quicklime). Made by heating calcium carbonate to drive off the carbon dioxide. It contains from 2-10% water, 80-95% lime, 1-5% carbon dioxide, and minor quantities of magnesium, aluminum, iron, and silicon. (1)

calcium oxide-hydrated: (hydrated lime, water-slaked lime). Made by treating burned lime with just enough water to slake, or hydrate, it. It contains from 20-30% water, 60-80% lime, and impurities similar to burned lime. (1)

calcium phosphate: Calcium salts of phosphoric acid that occur in the following common forms: monocalcium phosphate, dicalcium phosphate, tricalcium phosphate and apatite. Only monocalcium phosphate is water soluble. Dicalcium phosphate is citrate soluble and tricalcium phosphate and apatite are insoluble. (1,2)

calcium sulfate: (gypsum, land plaster). Made by treating lime or calcium phosphate with sulfuric acid. It is often recommended where it is necessary to add calcium to the soil without altering the pH. (1)

caliper: Diameter of a tree trunk measured six inches above the ground. If the caliper is greater than four inches, another measurement is taken twelve inches above the ground.

callus: Simple, undifferentiated tissue that develops during wound-healing. The hard, knobby outgrowth on some tree trunks. The downward extension of the lemma in some grasses. Also, the thickened lower joint and first glume in *Eriochloa.* (4,10,16)

calyx: All the sepals of a flower. (4)

cambium: The lateral meristem that increases the diameter of stems and roots in vascular plants by producing the xylem, phloem, and cortex of the stem and trunk. (4)

candle: The new growth of a needled conifer. (19)

cane: The main stem of a shrub, usually a berry plant or rose. In grapes, the new, current-year's shoots after hardening and autumn leaf-drop. (4)

cane cutter: See bramble hook.

canescent: Covered with a grayish-white film formed by a coating of fine hairs. (11)

cane-type: A type of orchid that has coarse, upright stems that resemble those of sugarcane and are strong, yet fleshy.

canker: A necrotic symptom of a disease in woody plants where the dead area is sharply defined by disfigured bark surrounded by callus. (4)

Cape: (Cape bulbs). Bulbous or tuberous plants originally from the area around the Cape of Good Hope, among them *Gladiolus, Freesia, Amaryllis, Ixia,* and *Sparaxis*. (10)

capillary mat: A synthetic fiber mat placed on top of a watertight membrane on a flat bench and used as a means of watering small pots.

capillary water: Water held in the soil against the force of gravity by capillary forces and representative of the total amount of water available to the plant. (4)

caprification: Pollination of the flower of certain figs by a special wasp. (9)

capsule: A simple, dry, dehiscent fruit with numerous carpels, as in Jimsonweed. (14)

carbamate: Organic derivative of carbamic acid used in fungicides, insecticides, and herbicides. (17)

carbon-nitrogen (C/N) ratio: The ratio obtained by dividing the percentage of carbon by the percentage of nitrogen in organic materials. (1)

carinate: Keeled. (16)

carotene: A yellow pigment and precursor of vitamin A. (17)

carpel: The part of the pistil containing the ovule, or seeds. Some pistils are composed of more than one carpel. (4,14)

caryopsis: An indehiscent fruit with the pericarp fused to the seed. The grain of the grasses. (16)

cassino: A simple summer garden shelter. (11)

castor pumice: The ground residue of castor beans minus the oil. It contains about 5% nitrogen, 2% phosphorus, 1% potassium and 93% organic matter. (2)

catch-crop: A crop of secondary importance used to occupy the ground between two or more main crops. (11)

catchment basin: Drainage area. (8)

cation: A positively charged ion. For example, calcium (Ca^{++}), magnesium (Mg^{++}), sodium (Na^+), potassium (K^+), and hydrogen (H^+). (1)

cation exchange capacity: (CEC). The milliequivalents of cations per 100 grams of soil which can be held by surface forces and which can be replaced by other cations. (1)

catkin: (ament). The elongate cluster of either female or male flowers on certain species, such as walnuts and willow. (9)

cattleya: A type of orchid.

caulescent: Having a stem. (11)

caustic lime: See lime.

CB: In melons, the disease resistance code for crown blight.

cellulose: A structural material in the cell walls of plants. (8)

cement: Any substance used as a binder for other materials. In masonry, the term usually refers to Portland cement, a substance containing the oxides, sulphates, and carbonates of silicon, iron, aluminum, calcium, and magnesium. This cement is used extensively in making mortar and concrete. Other cements include various adhesives and epoxy glues. (8)

certified plant: A plant produced under strict guidelines and inspected by a nonbiased regulatory agency to ensure trueness to name and freedom from pests and damage. (4)

chaff: The thin, brittle bracts of flowers, as in everlastings and grasses. (10)

chain: A measurement now little used. One chain = 100 links = four rods (poles) = 66 feet. Eighty chains equal one mile. (8)

chalking: In tulips, the development of chalklike spots on stored plants. (9)

chelate: (sequestering agent). An organic compound able to hold a plant nutrient, usually a trace element, in a form which prevents it from binding with other elements in the soil, thus keeping it available for plant use. Without chelates, iron, copper, manganese, and zinc all become insoluble in soil. (1,2)

chilling injury: Exposure of cold-sensitive plants or plant parts to temperatures above freezing but below the temperatures they normally experience, as in bananas browning when exposed to refrigerator temperatures. (9)

chilling requirement: The number of hours at or below a baseline temperature that is needed to cause certain physiologic changes that result in resumption of the normal growth sequence following the cold period. (4)

chimera: A plant or plant part having tissues of varying genetic makeup growing next to each other. (4,10)

chitting: See fluid drilling. The treatment given to seed whereby it is germinated beforehand and planted in the field as a slurry.

chloride: (muriate). A salt of hydrochloric acid. Many species of plants are highly sensitive to this salt. (1)

chlorinated hydrocarbons: (chlorinated organics, chlorinateds). That group of insecticides containing chlorine, carbon, hydrogen, and sometimes oxygen. The group contains DDT and chlordane and its former widespread use has been curtailed. (17)

chlorophyll: The green pigment in plants necessary for photosynthesis. (4)

chloroplast: Structures within the cells of green plants that contain the chlorophyll and in which photosynthesis is carried on. (8)

chlorosis: The yellowing of the green portions of a plant caused by a reduction in chlorophyll; usually refers to the leaves. (1,4)

C horizon: The layer of soil beneath the B horizon. It has relatively little biological activity. (14)

chromosome: A unit within the nucleus of a cell that transmits hereditary characteristics. (17)

ciliate: Fringed with hairs. (15)

cion: See scion.

cladode: A flattened stem, as in cactus, that functions as a leaf.

cladophyll: A small branch resembling a leaf or bract, as those occurring on the spears of asparagus. (17)

clasping: The state wherein a stalkless leaf partly or wholly surrounds a twig, as in the New England aster. (11)

clavate: Club-shaped. (15)

claw: A long, narrow, basal part of the petal in such flowers as roses, irises, and pinks. (10)

clay: A soil particle less than 0.002 millimeters in diameter. (1,3)

claypan: A compact, rather impermeable layer of clay in the subsoil that restricts water and root penetration. (14)

clean cultivation: Maintaining the soil in a weed-free condition by repeated tilling or hoeing.

cleft graft: A procedure generally done in topworking. The stock is split and two scions are inserted into each split near the bark or the stock so that both cambia come in contact.

cleistogamous: Flowers that are fertilized without opening. (16)

climber: A type of rose that produces large, everblooming flowers on climbing stems.

cloche: A small tent, formerly of glass but now usually made of paper or plastic, used for covering plants individually or in a row as protection against frost, cold, wind, etc. (10)

clod: A compact, compressed lump of soil usually produced by working land that is either too wet or too dry. (3)

clone: (clon). A group of genetically identical, vegetatively propagated plants all descended from the same individual. (4)

clove: A division of a separated bulb, as in garlic. (10)

clubmoss: A group of plants containing the lycopodiums and the resurrection plants. They are useful for wreaths and other decorations. (8)

clubroot: (finger and toe disease). A swelling of the roots of crucifers caused by a slime mold. (10,11)

clump: A cluster of shrubs; a mass of rootstocks considered for division. (10)

CMV: In spinach and cucumbers, the disease resistance code for cucumber mosaic virus (blight).

coalescent: Having two or more parts united. (15)

cobblestone: A rounded rock between eight and 25 centimeters in diameter. (3)

cocoa shell meal: Ground husks of the cacao seed. It contains about 2.5% nitrogen, 1% phosphorus, 3% potassium and 84% organic matter. It is used as a fertilizer conditioner and as a fertilizer itself. (2)

cold frame: A bottomless outdoor growing structure covered with removable glass or transparent plastic and heated only by the sun. It is used for hardening, forcing plants, and for growing transplants. (6,10)

cole crop: A crop belonging to the *Brassica* genus, including broccoli, cabbage, cauliflower, kohlrabi, rutabaga, and Brussels sprouts. (9,10)

coleoptile: The first leaf protecting the shoot apex and plumule from damage by soil particles during germination in some monocots. (14)

collar: Flared tissue at the base of a branch.

collarettes: A type of dahlia that produces flowers with a single row of ray florets and one or more rows of petaloids, often of a different color, arranged in a collar around the disk. (10)

colloid: Soil particles having a diameter ranging from 0.02 to 0.005 microns. They have a high base exchange and are small enough to remain suspended in a liquid without agitation. (1)

column: The structure in orchids formed by the fused stamens and pistils in the center of the flower.

companion cropping: Planting more than one crop on the same land at the same time. This may include intercropping, nurse cropping, and succession planting. (10)

compatible: Free from any condition that would prevent pollen grains from functioning normally on a pistil, or graft unions from forming normally. (4)

complete fertilizer: A fertilizer containing all three of the major fertilizer nutrients (nitrogen, phosphorus, and potassium). It also may, or may not, contain the minor nutrients. (1)

complete flower: A flower having all parts, i.e., pistil, stamen, petals, and sepals. (4)

compost: (artificial manure, synthetic manure). The rotted remains of organic debris. Usually, compost is made from plant material with a relatively low carbon to nitrogen ratio. Straw, sawdust, cornstalks and wood chips, high in cellulose and low in nitrogen, do not decompose readily. However, they will rot rapidly under warm, moist, slightly alkaline, aerobic conditions if nitrogen fertilizer is added. Also, the term can refer to a potting mix for container-grown plants, especially in Europe. (2,3)

compression wood: Dense reaction wood in conifers formed on the lower sides of the branches. (19)

concrete: A mix of aggregates bound into a solid mass by cement. Ordinary concrete weighs about 163 pounds per cubic foot (two tons per cubic yard). Some common mixes are (cement:sand:stone) 1:2:3, 1:2:4, 1:2.5:4, 1:3:5. (8)

cone: The flower and fruit of a conifer. Also, more loosely, any cone-shaped fruit, such as that of magnolia and hops. (10)

conifer: A tree bearing woody cones with naked seeds, as a pine or spruce. (7)

container gardening: Growing plants in containers outdoors. (19)

contour: A line on the surface of the earth whereon all points are at the same elevation. (8)

controlled-release fertilizer: (delayed-release fertilizer, slow-release fertilizer, controlled-availibility fertilizer, slow-acting fertilizer, and metered-release fertilizer). The controlled dissolution of fertilizer at less than the rate of conventional water-soluble fertilizers.

coolhouse: A section of the greenhouse kept cooler than the rest for the growth of certain plants such as agaves and bay trees. (11)

copperas crystals: See iron sulfate.

copper sulfate: (bluestone, blue vitriol). A common copper salt used in fertilizers and pesticides. It contains about 31% copper. (1,2)

coppice: A small woodland, especially one containing second growth trees. (8)

copse: A small grove of trees. (8)

cordate: Heart-shaped. (11)

cordon: A tree or vine in which the growth is restricted by pruning to a single main stem bearing the spurs. (13)

cork: The cork of commerce is the bark of the cork oak, a tree indigenous to Spain and Portugal. (8)

corm: A globe-shaped, modified underground stem with terminal and lateral buds, as in the *Gladiolus* and crocus. (5)

cormel: A young corm arising from the base of older ones. (10)

corolla: A collective term referring to all the petals of a flower. (4)

corona: A bell-shaped outgrowth on the petals of some flowers.

corymb: A flat-topped flower cluster wherein the outer flowers open first. (15)

cottonseed meal: A by-product of cottonseed milling. The ground press cake with oil extracted contains about 5% nitrogen, 3% phosphoric acid, and 1% potassium. About 20% of the nitrogen is in the form of chitin which has no fertilizer value. (1,2)

cotyledon: The first leaf of a germinating seed, sometimes called the seed leaf. It may store food or develop with photosynthetic organs as the seed germinates.

coulure: The failure of grape flowers to set fruit.

coursonne: A small, short, fruiting lateral in fruit trees.

cover crop: A temporary crop used to cover the ground and prevent erosion, conserve nutrients, smother weeds, or improve the soil. This crop is eventually plowed under as green manure. (10)

crazy paving: Pavement made of irregularly shaped flagstones fitted to each other in random patterns without dressing. (11)

creeper: Plants or vines that grow close to the ground or cling to supporting structures by rootlets or tendrils. (8)

crenate: A leaf having margins with rounded teeth, especially if the teeth point toward the apex. (11)

creosote: A product of wood distillation formerly used widely as a wood preservative and disinfectant. (8)

crest: A ridge on a flower lying above and protecting the stigma; often applied to irises. (12)

cross-compatible: When the pollen of one cultivar is capable of growing on the stigma of another. (9)

cross-fruitful: Bearing fruit by cross-pollination.

cross-pollination: The transfer of pollen from the anther of one plant to the pistil of a plant of a different clone. (4)

crotch: The angle formed by the joining of two branches or of a branch and the trunk.

crown: The base of a perennial plant. The top of a tree (canopy). The area between stem and root (collar). (4,10)

crown bud: A flower bud formed under conditions that are often not suitable for flower bud formation. Buds below a crown bud remain vegetative. (6)

crown gall: A bacterial disease that causes swellings on the crowns of some plants such as raspberry, rose, and daisy. (11)

crown rot: A disease, caused by a fungus, that rots the lower stem and root of a number of plants such as aconite, cosmos, hosta, iris, and violet. (11)

crucifer: A plant in the mustard family. (10)

crumb: In soil, a soft, irregular particle from one to five millimeters in diameter. (14)

cucurbit: A plant in the Cucurbitaceae or squash family. These include pumpkins, squashes, gourds, melons, and cucumbers. (9)

cul-de-sac: A French term for a short street open only at one end. (8)

culm: The stem of a grass, sedge, and bamboo. (8,14)

cultigen: A plant or group of plants that exist only under cultivation, such as the seedless watermelon. (15)

cultival: An obscure form of the word "cultivar."(8)

cultivar: A *culti*vated *var*iety, as distinguished from a botanical variety. (4)

cultural control: The control of plant pests using cultivation practices. (19)

culturing: A laboratory technique to test for the presence of fungi or bacteria in a given plant.

cuneate: Wedge-shaped. (15)

curd: The edible flower head of broccoli and cauliflower, though usually used when referring to the latter. (10)

cure: Preparing a crop for storage, such as drying onion bulbs. (14)

cut flower: A plant grown for the display of its flowers in vases or arrangements. (19)

cuticle: The layer of waxy substance covering the aboveground parts of plants. (17)

cuttage: The production of cuttings. (10)

cutting: A detached plant part used for propagation. (14)

cutting rot: A disease of *Pelargonium* and coleus characterized by a dark-colored rot on the stem near the soil line. (10)

cycad: Palmlike plants used for ornament in warm climates. (8)

cymbidium: A type of orchid.

cyme: A flat-topped flower cluster with the center flowers opening first. (15)

cytokinin: A group of natural and synthetic hormones that stimulate cell division, branching, and bud initiation and retard abscission and senescence. (4)

cytoplasm: The transparent liquid making up the entire protoplasm of a cell, with the exception of the nucleus. (17)

D

daily flow irrigation: Trickle irrigation. (19)

damping-off: The condition wherein certain pathogens cause the lower portion of the stem of young seedlings to rot. (5)

dard: A bud surrounded by a leafy rosette. A short lateral shoot less than three inches in length, ending in a flower bud. (9,13)

day-neutral: A plant that flowers independent of the length of day or night. (4)

deacclimation: Loss of adaptation to climate. Often interchangeable with dehardening. (4)

dead man: A block of concrete, metal, or wood buried in the soil and attached by a cable to a wall or other structure to serve as an anchor. (8)

deciduous: The property of shedding of parts at the end of the season. Deciduous plants drop their leaves at the end of the growing season. (4)

decline: The gradual weakening of a plant. (19)

decorticated: In beets, the removal, usually by rubbing, of the fruit coat of the seed ball, resulting in better germination, less need to thin, easier planting, and a greater number of seed per pound.

decumbent: The growth habit of a plant in which the lower parts of the stems lie close to the ground without rooting, while the upper part is erect. (4)

defoliant: A chemical that causes the leaves of a plant to drop. (14)

degree-day: A unit of heat representing one degree above a given average daily base value, usually the minimum temperature for growth of the plant. (4)

dehiscence: The opening of a fruit, anther or other plant part along definite lines. (4)

dehorn: See buckhorn.

dehulled: The condition in seed of having the glumes, pods, or other outside covering removed. (14)

delayed-release fertilizer: See controlled-release fertilizer.

deliquescent: Able to absorb moisture from the air and liquify. (2)

dendrobium: A type of orchid.

denitrification: The reduction of nitrates to nitrites, ammonia, and free or gaseous nitrogen, usually by microbial activity. (1,3)

dentate: Toothed. (15)

desiccant: A compound applied to plant tissue to speed drying. (14)

desucker: The removal of undesirable shoots from a plant. (19)

determinate: Having a defined growth limit. The uniform flowering of a plant within a certain time period, resulting in maturation of all fruit at about the same time. (4,14)

dethatch: The removal of thatch from a lawn.

dew: Atmospheric moisture condensed onto surfaces when the temperature drops below the dew point. (8)

dew point: The temperature below which atmospheric moisture condenses into droplets. Cold air can hold less water than warm air and as the temperature drops, the relative humidity of the air increases until, at 100%, the dew point is reached and water vapor becomes ice or water, depending upon the temperature. (8)

D hoe: See Dutch hoe.

diageotropic: Horizontal growth.

diammonium phosphate: A fertilizer containing nitrogen and phosphorus. The fertilizer grade contains 18% to 21% nitrogen and from 46% to 54% phosphorus. (2)

diatomaceous earth: This fluffy gray-white material is composed of the remains of microscopic algae called diatoms. It is used as a fertilizer conditioner and as a pesticide. (2)

dibble: (dibber). A thin, pencil-shaped tool used to make the planting hole for seedlings. It varies in size according to the size of the plant. (5)

dicalcium phosphate: The di-calcic salt of phosphoric acid. (1,2)

dichasium: An inflorescence type.

dichogamy: Maturation of male and female parts of the flower at different times, preventing self-pollination. (14)

dicotyledon: (dicot). A class of flowering plants having embryos with two cotyledons. (14)

dieback: The progressive death of a shoot from the tip backwards; this symptom may be indicative of disease or environmental damage. (11)

dihybrid cross: The cross of parents differing in two characteristics. (14)

diluent: An inert substance used to dilute the active ingredient of a pesticide, fertilizer, etc. (14)

dimension stone: Quarried rock which has been sized and shaped for use in construction. (8)

dioecious: Male and female flowers occurring on different plants of the same species, as in some hollies.

diploid: A plant having two sets of chromosomes.

direct seeding: To sow seed in the area in which the plants will grow, as opposed to transplanting.

dirt band: A small, bottomless and topless paper pot used to start seedlings; now mostly replaced by some form of peat pot. (11)

disbud: To remove a flower bud. (5)

disc: (disk). The flattened end of the receptacle that bears the flowers in the heads of members of the composite family. The flattened end of some tendrils. Also, to use a disc-harrow in soil preparation. (10)

disc harrow: An implement with upright discs dragged over the land by horse or tractor to break clods and level the field.

diurnal: Recurring every day. (14)

division: Propagation of plants by separating portions of the clump, rhizome, etc. In plant classification, the ranking between kingdom and class designated by names ending in *-phyta.* (10,19)

DM: In spinach, cucumbers, and melons, the disease resistance code for downy mildew.

dogtrot: See breezeway.

dolomite: A naturally occurring mineral of calcium and magnesium carbonate used as a liming material and in fertilizers as a neutralizing agent. (1,2)

dormancy: Temporary suspension of plant growth due to external or internal factors. (4)

dormant eye: A budded rose plant wherein the dormant bud (eye) is not allowed to grow prior to shipment. (6)

dormant oil: A highly refined oil sprayed on plants during the dormant season to kill overwintering insects or their eggs.

dormant spray: A chemical spray applied during the late fall, winter, or early spring season. (18)

double digging: Removing the soil from a row to spade depth, breaking up the soil remaining in the bottom of the trench, adding humus to the trench, then filling the trench with topsoil from an adjacent row. This soil column should be inverted when placed into the trench.

double fertilization: The fusions of a sperm and egg and a second sperm with the two polar nuclei. (19)

double leader: The two main stems on a tree. (19)

double potting: Positioning a potted plant into a larger pot lined with sphagnum moss. (19)

double superphosphate: (superphosphate, treble superphosphate, triple superphosphate, multiple superphosphate). A fertilizing compound containing 40-50% available phosphoric acid and differing from normal superphosphate by containing little calcium sulfate. (1)

double-work: In grafting, the situation in which the scion and the stock of a tree are separated by an interstock so that the tree has been grafted twice and thus has three parts.

drain tile: Concrete, ceramic, or plastic pipe placed to shunt water from the soil. (3)

drawn: Seedlings or plants that are thin and leggy. (11)

dressing: The trimming of nursery stock for future operations such as propagation. Application of manure, topsoil, fertilizer, etc., over the land to improve crop growth. (10,11)

dried blood: The dried and ground blood of slaughtered animals. It contains about 12% nitrogen. One ton of dried blood is collected from about 300 slaughtered cattle. (2)

dried manure: The dried dung, urine, and bedding of animals. Most of the fecal nutrients are insoluble and must be decomposed before becoming available to the plant. The nutrients in urine are quickly available to the plant. Most of the urinary nitrogen is present as urea and most of the manure itself is humus. (2)

drill: To plant seeds in a furrow. The furrow in which seeds are planted. (9,10)

drill hole fertilization: To fertilize trees by punching holes in the soil beneath the drip line and filling them with fertilizer. (19)

drip irrigation: (trickle irrigation). A method whereby water is applied slowly to the soil surface through small-orificed emitters. (3)

dripline: An imaginary line on the ground around the tree beneath the tips of the branches.

drip tip: The pointed tip of a leaf that aids in draining water from the blade surface.

drupe: A simple, fleshy fruit from a single carpel and composed of a skin, a fleshy portion, and a stone, such as an olive, peach, and plum. (4)

druplet: A small drupe, usually in aggregate fruit such as raspberry. (4)

dryad: A shade-loving plant. (8)

dry off: To gradually reduce the amount of water. To lay pots on their sides in the shade to prepare bulbs for ripening or plants for resting between periods of forcing. (7)

dry wall: A wall of stone layed without mortar. Also, Sheetrock used in building construction. (8)

duff: Partially decomposed organic matter found beneath plants, including leaves, fruit, etc. (4)

duplex: In dahlias, similar to singles but with two rows of outer petals and an open center.

dust mulch: A fine, loose, dry layer of soil produced by cultivation to reduce the amount of water evaporating from lower levels of the soil. (8)

dutch bulbs: Any of the hardy bulbs planted in fall for spring bloom, such as tulips, narcissi, crocus, etc. (11)

Dutch hoe: (English scuffle hoe, D hoe). An implement for weeding between plant rows. The rectangular blade is sharpened on both long sides and is set at an angle to the handle. The gardener slides the hoe forward and back in a scuffling manner. (10)

dwarf: A plant that attains a height less than that of a plant in the same species without the dwarfing characteristic.

E

earlywood: (springwood). The first-formed, less dense wood of an annual growth ring. (14)

earthing-up: Mounding soil around the roots of plants to reduce tuber sunburn, as in potato, to increase root hold, as in corn, or to blanch celery, etc. (11)

eave: The overhang of a roof beyond a sidewall. (5)

ecology: The study of all life relative to the environment. (14)

ecosystem: All factors in a living community and the surrounding nonliving environment. (14)

ecotype: A genetic variation of a plant within a species that is well-adapted to a particular environment. (14)

edaphic: Pertaining to the soil and its influence upon plant growth. (3)

edging: Defining the edge of a bed, border, path, driveway, etc., by cutting a vertical edge in the turf, by placement of plastic, masonry, or a metal strip, or by planting a border of flowers, hedges, etc. (11)

edging plant: A plant used as edging, usually a low-growing species such as dwarf barberry, myrtle, and candytuft. (11)

eelworm: Nematode.

emulsifiable concentrate: Liquid formulation of a pesticide that forms an emulsion upon the addition of water. (17)

emulsion: A mixture in which oily, fatty, or resinous material is suspended in a liquid. (11)

encapsulated fertilizer: A fertilizer made up of nutrient granules embedded in a synthetic resin which dissolves slowly, releasing the nutrients over an extended period of time. A slow-release fertilizer. (19)

endemic: The term used to describe plants indigenous to an area. Opposite of "exotic."(11)

endocarp: The innermost layer of the fruit wall, such as the hard pit in a cherry.

endodermis: A sheath enclosing vascular bundles in roots. (17)

endosperm: The stored food in a seed. (17)

English scuffle hoe: See Dutch hoe.

enology: The study of winemaking. (4)

entomology: The study of insects. (18)

epicotyl: The upper part of a seedling between the cotyledons and the first true leaves. (14)

epidermis: The skin; the outer layer of cells surrounding all young plant organs. (19)

epigeal: The condition in seed germination in which the cotyledons are lifted above the soil line, as in beans. (17)

epigyny: A flower type wherein the sepals, stamens, and petals appear to grow from the ovary top. That is, they appear to be positioned above (*epi-*) the ovary (*-gyny*). (19)

epinasty: The twisting of a stem or leaf, usually, the downward bending of a leaf. (14)

epiphyte: (air plant). A plant which grows upon another but is not a parasite. Commonly, these are tropical plants such as orchids, aroids, and some ferns. (8,10)

epsom salts: See magnesium sulfate.

equivalent acidity: The calcium carbonate equivalent of the acidic residue of a fertilizer. A measure of how acid a fertilizer is. (1)

equivalent basicity: See alkaline-forming.

espalier: A plant, often a fruit tree, trained to grow flat against a wall or trellis. (8)

essential plant nutrient: One of 16 nutrients required by growing crops for normal development. (1)

ethylene: A naturally occurring hormonal gas that promotes ripening of fruit and flowering in some plants. (4)

etiolation: The process of developing small leaves, stretched stems and chlorosis in the absence of light or under the conditions of low light intensity. (4)

evapotranspiration: The loss of water from plants and soil; a combination of *evapo*ration and *transpiration.*

evening garden: A garden containing plants grown for their fragrance or for attributes other than visual. Supplemental lighting may or may not be used. (11)

everbearing: (fallbearing). In small fruit, the production of more than one crop in a given season.

evergreen: A plant that retains its foliage throughout the year. Conifers, most hollies, and rhododendrons are common examples. (8)

evergreen garden: A garden composed entirely or primarily of evergreens. In the north, these are mostly the conifers; in the south, a mixture of conifers and broad-leaved evergreens. (11)

everlasting: A flower that has a papery quality and holds its color and shape throughout the winter. (7,10)

exocarp: The outermost layer of the fruit wall. The skin of peach, cherry, and olive. (19)

exotic: Not indigenous or native. (11)

eye: A common term for a bud; the dark center of flowers such as the black-eyed Susan; the sunken buds of the Irish potato. (4,5,11)

F

F: (FW). In tomatoes and melons, the disease resistance code for fusarium wilt. The number following refers to the race of the pathogen.

F_1: The first filial generation resulting from a cross between two parents. (14)

F_2: The second filial generation resulting from a cross of two F_1 parents. (14)

fairy ring: A conspicuous circular area surrounded by mushrooms, often of the species *Marasimus oreades*. Any ring of vegetation in sharp contrast with its surroundings. (8)

falcate: Sickle-shaped. (15)

fall: One of the three outer segments of an iris flower. (11,12)

fallbearing: See everbearing.

fallow: To allow land to rest without being planted for a year or more after a crop has been harvested. It is practiced to accumulate moisture in dry areas. (10)

fan: In pruning, a tree in which all branches are trained from a short trunk into a fan-shaped pattern and attached to a wall. (13)

fasciation: An abnormal enlargement and flattening of stems. The condition is common in *Nicotiana, Celosia,* and *Lilium. (*9,10)

fastigiate: Having compact, erect branches. (15)

fast-release fertilizer: A fertilizer that contains nutrients immediately available to the plant. (19)

feather: A lateral shoot on current year's wood. (13)

feather maiden tree: A one year old, branched tree in the nursery.

feeder roots: Fine roots that appear at the ends of the root system and that are responsible for most of the uptake of nutrients and water. (4)

ferrous sulfate: See iron sulfate.

fertigation: Application of fertilizer through irrigation water. (3)

fertilization: The union of egg and sperm to produce a zygote. Union of sperm and polar nuclei to produce endosperm. Application of soil amendments to increase fertility and improve plant growth. (4)

fertilizer: Any material that contains one or more of the essential nutrients in liquid or dry form and is applied to plants to enhance growth and development. (1,3)

fertilizer burn: The burnlike damage to plants caused by excessive application of fertilizer, or the application of fertilizer too close to the plant roots. It is most likely to occur with fast-release materials. (19)

fertilizer grade: The minimum amount of nutrients guaranteed in a fertilizer. Total nitrogen (not ammonia), available phosphoric acid, and water-soluble potassium are expressed as percentages of the blend. (1,2)

fertilizer ratio: The ratio of nitrogen:phosphate:potassium in a fertilizer. It is expressed in the lowest common denominator such as 1:2:2 (5-10-10) or 1:1:1 (10-10-10). (3)

fibrous roots: A root system in which both main and lateral roots have similar diameters.

field capacity: Amount of water remaining in the soil after all free water has drained away. Usually, the amount remaining two to three days after a soaking rain or substantial irrigation. (3)

field hoe: A heavy type of common hoe.

field percentage: The maximum amount of capillary water available to the plant. (19)

filament: The stalk of the stamen that supports the anther. (4)

filiform: Threadlike. (16)

filler: Material added to fertilizer and some pesticides to increase the volume. (19)

fimbriate: Fringed. (16)

finger and toe disease: See clubroot.

fire: (fire disease). Botrytis blight of tulips. (11)

fire blight: A bacterial disease attacking members of the rose family, especially the pear. (10)

firefang: To become dried or scorched from heat produced during decomposition, especially in reference to grains and manure.

fish scrap: Prepared from nonedible fish and offal from canneries. The raw material is steamed, pressed to remove the oil, dried, and ground. It has some value as a fertilizer in the home garden, and contains about 9% nitrogen, 7% phosphorus, 1% potassium, 8% calcium, and 70% organic matter. (2)

fixation: The process rendering nutrients, usually potassium, phosphorus, micronutrients, and ammonia, unavailable or fixed in the soil. The process by which atmospheric nitrogen is combined into a form useful for plant growth. (1)

flagstone: A thin fragment, 15 to 38 centimeters long, of sandstone, slate, shale, limestone, or, sometimes, schist, often used for paving or as stepping stones. (3,8)

flake: In carnations, a flower striped with a single color. (11)

flat: A tray made of wood or plastic, about 15 inches by 20 inches by 3 inches, used for raising small plants from seed, or for carrying potted plants. (5)

flocculate: To clump together, especially in reference to soil particles. (14)

floral tube: A tube formed by the fused bases of the sepals, petals, and stamens that envelopes the ovary. (4)

floret: Small, individual flowers that make up a dense inflorescence, such as the spikelet of a grass. (4)

floribunda: A type of rose that bears flowers in clusters continuously and profusely. The flowers closely resemble hybrid teas.

floricane: The fruiting cane of a bramble during the season of flowering, i.e., the season after it was produced. (4)

floriculture: The cultivation of flowering and other herbaceous ornamental plants. (18)

florigen: The group of several compounds that are thought to be involved in the formation of flower buds.

flower: The reproductive organ of a seed-bearing plant. (18)

fluid drilling: Planting pre-germinated seeds that are contained in a protective gelatinous substance. (17)

foliage plant: Herbaceous plants, trees, and shrubs grown for the beauty of their form, texture, and growth habit rather than for their flowers.

foliar analysis: Analysis of the foliage and/or shoots to determine nutrient status of the plant.

foliar diagnosis: Examination of the chemical composition of selected plant parts, their color and growth to estimate mineral nutrient deficiencies. (3)

foliar feeding: To apply nutrients to the foliage of plants. (19)

follicle: A simple, dry, single-carpeled, dehiscent fruit, such as that of milkweed. (14)

forb: Any herbaceous plant, excluding grass, found in grasslands or open woodlands. (8)

forcing: Making plants or bulbs bloom out of their normal season or making them bloom in a shorter length of time than normally required. (7)

fork: A narrow angle between the branches, roots, or shoots of a plant.

forma: A category of classification in which the members vary only slightly from the parent species. (19)

formal garden: A garden with geometric and balanced design wherein the beauty of the plant material is secondary to its usefulness in the overall design. (11)

foundation planting: Plant material arranged along the foundation of a building to hide the foundation and/or to accent or soften certain other features of the building. (11)

foxy: The smell of the American bunch grape, typified by 'Concord.'(4)

fragipan: Dense, brittle layer of soil resulting from compaction. It is nearly impervious to water and root penetration. (8)

frame: The abbreviation for coldframe. (11)

friable: Crumbly. A term referring to the crumbliness of the soil. (3)

frog spittle: (snake spit). The foamy mass found in summer on grass or other low growing plants, often thought to have been produced by frogs or snakes, but really the secretion of the spittle bug. (11)

frond: The large, compound leaf of a fern or palm. (8)

frost: See hoarfrost.

frost action: (frost boil). The action of frost on the soil. This includes soil expansion, soil softening during thaws, which, when it occurs in the subgrade can cause cracks in pavement (frost boil), and frost heaving of plants and posts. (8)

frost heaving: (heaving). An upward or lateral movement of the soil and/or plants caused by the expansion of soil water during freezing. (3)

frost pocket: A low area into which cold air settles, making frost more likely.

frost seed: Seeding hardy species of seed, such as clover, spinach, peas, etc., in early spring to allow the frost action to work them into the soil. It is sometimes done on snow or directly over a cover crop.

fruit: A ripened ovary usually containing seeds and accessory parts. In common usage, a fruit is a seed-bearing structure usually eaten raw, as a side dish or as dessert, and produced as a perennial.

fruit bud: In fruit bearing plants, a term synonomous with "flower buds."(4)

fruiting body: The structure in which fungal spores are borne. (11)

fruiting wood: Shoots bearing flower buds and/or fruit.

fruit set: The swelling and initial development of the ovary into a fruit. (9)

frutescent: Shrub-like. (8)

fully sugary enhanced: See sugary enhanced +.

fumigant: A gaseous substance used to control pests in the soil and in greenhouses.

fumigate: To control pests through the use of toxic fumes produced by a fumigant. (11)

fungicide: A chemical substance that kills fungi. (17)

furrow: An opening remaining in the soil after the furrow slice has been turned out by a plow. (3)

fusiform: Spindle-shaped. (16)

G

gall: A swollen, abnormal growth of plant tissue around the eggs or larvae of insects or in response to the attack of certain pathogens. (8)

gamete: A cell having the ability to fuse with another cell to create a new individual. Sperm and eggs are gametes.

garden: An area of special development containing plants, such as a park or arboretum, or of special use, such as a flower garden or vegetable garden. (18)

gazebo: A Dutch term for a summer house or garden shelter that enjoys a beautiful view. It is somewhat raised, though not on a hill, and originally commanded a view overlooking the garden wall. (8,11)

gene: A segment of DNA that carries the specific hereditary characters of an individual organism. (19)

genetic dwarf: A plant that is dwarfed because of its particular genetic makeup and not because of the influence of a size-controlling rootstock or of cultural practices.

genotype: The genetic makeup of a plant.

genus: A group of closely related organisms more specific than the family and less specific than the species. *pl.* genera. (8)

geophyte: According to some plant classifications, a plant that lives with its buds buried in the soil, as bulbs. (8)

geotropism: (gravitropism). The response of plant growth to the forces of gravity. Roots are generally positively geotropic, since they grow in a downward direction, while shoots are generally negatively geotropic.

germination: The beginning of growth in a seed, spore, or pollen grain. (8)

gibberellin: A group of hormones that affect seed germination, cell elongation, flower induction, and parthenocarpy. (4)

gibbous: Swollen on one side. (16)

girdling: Removal of a narrow ring of bark to affect fruit set, fruit size, and ripening (in grapes) or to induce the production of flower buds (in many other woody plants). Removal of a large ring of bark resulting in plant death. (4)

glabrous: Having no hairs. (11)

glasshouse: A European term for an artificially heated structure used for growing plants. Similar to greenhouse.

glaucous: Covered with a white, waxy bloom. (11)

glochid: A tiny, barbed bristle, often arranged in tufts, as on some cacti.

glumes: The pair of bracts at the base of a grass spikelet. (16)

gooseneck: The stage in narcissus when the unopened flower curves at a right angle to its axis. Flowers harvested prior to this stage will not bend or open properly. (9)

grading: The alteration of a slope.

graft: Insertion of a scion into a rootstock in such a manner that the two parts will knit and grow as a single unit. (4) Several kinds of grafts include bridge grafting, for repairing wounds to the bark; budding, the insertion of a bud and surrounding tissue beneath the bark of a stock, usually for changing the cultivar; approach, bark, brace, cleft, inarching, inlay, side, splice, veneer, and whip.

grafting compound: Grafting wax or a water-asphaltum mixture used to cover the wounds made during grafting. (9)

grafting wax: A mixture of beeswax, rosin, and raw linseed oil in the proportion of 2:1:4 for hand wax. It is used to cover the wounds made during grafting to prevent desiccation of the union area. (9)

graft union: See bud union.

grandiflora: A type of rose that produces a single double flower borne on a long stem. The flowers are somewhat smaller than those of a hybrid tea.

granular fertilizer: Fertilizer in the form of particles usually between one and four millimeters in diameter. (3)

gravitational water: Loosely held, excess water that generally drains from soil within a short time period.

gravitropism: See geotropism.

greenhouse: A structure covered with a transparent material, such as glass or plastic, for the purpose of admitting natural light for plant growth. (18)

green manure: Crops grown primarily to be plowed under for the benefit of the soil and the following crop. Crops for this purpose commonly include alfalfa, vetch, buckwheat, clover, rye, and oats. (2,3)

greensand: A silicate of iron and potash. The potash is insoluble in water and only slightly available as a nutrient without special treatment. It contains about 6% potash, 1% phosphorus, 2% calcium, and 2% magnesium. (2)

green vitriol: See iron sulfate.

ground color: The background color of the skin of mature fruit. The fruit later often develops another color, called the over color, such as red in apple, which partially or completely covers the original ground, or green color. The general background color of plant parts.

ground cover: Low plants, excluding grasses, such as *Pachysandra* and lily of the valley, used to cover the soil in light traffic areas or where grass will not thrive. (9)

ground lime: See lime.

growing season: That period, expressed in days, ranging from the last spring frost to the first fall frost.

grow on: To continue growing a plant to a larger size. (5)

growth habit: The form of a plant.

growth regulator: One of many classes of natural or synthetic substances that control or alter plant growth. (4)

grub: The larvae of beetles inhabiting the soil. (19)

grub hoe: A heavy implement resembling a pickaxe but with one axe-like blade for cutting roots and another heavy hoe-like blade for slicing the soil. (11)

guano: A highly variable term generally used to describe the partially decomposed excrement of various animals such as seals, bats, and birds. It accumulates in areas with little rainfall and in caves. The term must be used with a modifier such as "bat (cave) guano" or "Peruvian (bird) guano." Bat guano contains about 6% nitrogen,

9% phosphorus, and 2% potassium, while Peruvian guano contains about 12% nitrogen, 11% phosphorus, and 2% potassium, along with about 12% calcium. Phosphatic guano is bird guano leached by rain. (2)

guttation: Water exuded through pores (hydathodes) at the tips of leaves, especially at night, as a result of root pressure. (4)

gymnosperm: A group of plants whose seeds are not enclosed in a seed case. This group includes the conifers and the cycads. (8)

gynoedioecious: A species with both perfect and pistillate flowers occurring on different plants.

gynoecious: A plant producing female flowers and therefore having the potential to produce more fruit than a normal type. The term is commonly used with cucumbers.

gynoecium: A collective term for the pistils of a flower.

gynomonoecious: A species with both perfect and pistillate flowers occurring on the same plants.

gypsum: See calcium sulfate.

H

habit: The manner of plant growth. (11)

haft: The narrow tissue at the base of a segment of perianth. A pasture. A knife handle. (12)

ha-ha: An English term for a sunken wall or fence which is not visable until it is reached. (11)

half-hardy: Plants that will not endure the extreme winter temperatures of a region. Half-hardy perennials may succumb to dieback after extreme winters or require special winter protection, and half-hardy annuals must be started indoors and set out only after the weather has warmed sufficiently. (11)

halophyte: A plant indigenous to salt marshes. (8)

hanged: The condition wherein a new transplant has died or been severely weakened by not having the soil tamped firmly around its roots, causing the roots to dry out. (10)

harden: (harden-off). To acclimate, usually by gradual exposure to colder and/or drier conditions.

hardiness: A quality in plants that enables them to resist cold or winter in a particular climate. (18)

hardiness zone map: A map developed by the U.S. Department of Agriculture based upon minimum temperatures recorded over a number of years in areas of North America. (18)

hardpan: A hard layer of soil through which roots, animals, and water cannot penetrate. (4)

hardwood: The wood of a dicotyledonous tree, which may or may not actually be soft.

hardy: Plants which thrive in a given environment and survive under commonly encountered winter conditions. Also, the ability to endure summer heat is sometimes included in this term. (11)

harrow: The smoothing and pulverizing of plowed land with one of several types of implements, such as a disc harrow, spike-toothed harrow, or spring-toothed harrow. The mechanical equivalent of raking the soil. (10)

haulm: Straw from the stalks of wheat or rye. More generally, stalks of any crop from which seeds are harvested. The term is also applied to any straw or litter. (11)

haustorium: The organ of a parasite that absorbs nutrients from a host after penetrating its tissues.

hazeltine: (hazeltine weeder). A hand-weeding implement with a thin, flat blade in the shape of a three-sided square about four inches long, used for fine weeding and the thinning of small plants.

head: The section of a trunk, as in grape, where the arms and cordons originate. Also, any tight flower cluster, such as those on the daisy and aster. The branches of a tree above the crotch. (4,10,13)

heading: The process wherein some plants, such as cabbage and broccoli, form heads. Also, a shortened term for "heading-back"(stubbing).

heading-back: Pruning a portion of the terminal growth of a branch.

headland: Open space at the ends of the rows and at the field border to facilitate the turning of equipment, cultural operations, etc. (4)

heartwood: The innermost layers of the xylem that are dead and crushed and often stained a deep brown or red. (4)

heaving: See frost heaving.

heavy metals: Dense metals. In agriculture these include copper, iron, manganese, molybdenum, cobalt, zinc, cadmium, mercury, nickel, and lead. The term usually connotes toxic materials detrimental to plant growth. (3)

heavy soil: A soil containing large amounts of clay. It is usually poorly drained and difficult to work.

hedge: A row of closely planted shrubs, usually kept continuously clipped and used as a divider or fence.

hedgerow: A dense planting of closely spaced trees that create a hedgelike effect.

hedging: Usually applied to the mechanical pruning of fruit trees in a hedgerow, where the tops and sides of the plants are clipped with tractor-mounted equipment.

heel: (heeling, heeling-in). To cover the roots of plants temporarily with soil or other medium to keep them from drying until planting. Also, a piece of older stem tissue left at the base of a cutting. (4,11)

hemiparasitic: A parasite that obtains water and minerals from its host.

herb: A plant with little woody tissue. More specifically, a plant used for medicine, food, flavor, or scent. (8)

herbaceous: Any plant without a persistent woody stem. The term is frequently applied to perennials whose tops die to the ground in the winter. (18)

herbaceous perennial: A type of plant wherein the aboveground portion dies back each fall, while the roots remain alive and regenerate the plant the following season.

herbicide: A chemical that kills plants. (4)

hermaphroditic: Having both sexes. (17)

hesperidium: A modified berry with a leathery rind, as in citrus.

heterosis: The condition of hybrid vigor wherein the offspring are more vigorous than the parents. (19)

heterozygous: Having differences in the gene pair.

hill: A planting system wherein plants are maintained as individuals with open ground around them, as in the hill system in strawberry culture. (4)

hilling: (hilling up). Mounding the soil around a plant to protect it from cold; to blanch it, as in celery and asparagus, to strengthen the stand of aerial-rooted plants, as in corn, or, to protect the shallow roots or tubers from sunburn, as in potatoes. (7)

hilum: The scar remaining on a seed where it was formerly attached to the seed stalk within the ovary. (19)

hip: The fruit of the rose. (15)

hoarfrost: (frost). The white frost that forms when the temperature falls below the dewpoint, which itself must be below freezing.

hoe: A tool for scraping and shallow cultivation which exists in several forms. The typical form is called a field or draw hoe. Others include the onion hoe, grub hoe, Dutch, bayonet hoe, ridging hoe, beet hoe, and the Warren-hoe.

holdfast: The apparatus, such as tendrils and pads, that allow a climbing vine to cling to vertical surfaces. (19)

homozygous: Having identical pairs of genes.

hopperburn: A condition caused by the leafhopper feeding on potato leaves, resulting in marginal browning and curling. (11)

hormone: An organic material produced in small quantities in one part of the plant and usually transported to another part where it affects growth. (4)

horticulture: The production and marketing of fruit, vegetables, and ornamental plants. (5)

hose-in-hose: The condition in a double flower, or where the calyx and the corolla are similarly colored, giving the appearance of one flower growing within another. It is found in azaleas, *Narcissus,* primroses, and Canterbury bells. (10)

host: A plant that provides sustenance for a parasite. (18)

hotbed: A structure for growing plants that is covered with glass or plastic and heated artificially. A heated coldframe.

hot cap: A semi-transparent paper or cardboard cone or box used as a temporary cover for plants in spring for frost and wind protection. (14)

hull: The outer shell of any fruit, often called the husk. More specifically, the calyx of the strawberry. (10)

humus: A decomposed and relatively stable complex dark brown or black component of the soil organic matter. It can contain fairly large amounts of nitrogen, phosphorus, sulfur, and other plant nutrients, in addition to carbon, hydrogen, and oxygen. It also aids the soil in retaining water and nutrients for plant use and makes up 20 to 50% of the organic matter in peat, compost, leaf mold, and rotted manure. The term is often used interchangeably with "soil organic matter."(1,2,3)

hurdle: A movable section of wooden fence used as a gate. (11)

hybrid: An individual plant resulting from the union of gametes differing in at least one characteristic. (4)

hybrid tea: The most common garden rose, characterized by flowers borne one to a stem or in clusters of three to five. The buds are long and pointed.

hybrid vigor: The enhanced growth and productivity displayed by a hybrid compared to its parents.

hydathode: A pore that excretes water, often at the tips or margins of leaves.

hydrated lime: See calcium oxide-hydrated and lime.

hydrophyte: A plant which normally grows in water or in saturated soil. (8)

hydroponics: (soilless gardening). Plant cultivation in water solutions containing nutrients and without soil. (8)

hydrotropism: The growth of a plant or plant part toward water.

hygroscopic: The ability to absorb atmospheric moisture, such as with common table salt. (1,2)

hygroscopic water: Water held very tightly in the soil by surface tension of the colloidal particles. This water is unavailable for plant growth. (8)

hylophyte: A plant indigenous to wet or damp woodlands. (8)

hypha: A threadlike filament; the structural unit of a fungus. All hyphae together compose the mycelium. (4)

hypobaric storage: The storage of plant material under reduced atmospheric pressure.

hypocotyl: The portion of an embryo or young plant that lies between the roots and the cotyledons. (19)

hypogeal: The type of seed germination in which the cotyledons remain below the soil surface, as in peas. (17)

hypogynous: The type of flower in which the stamens, petals, and sepals are attached below (*hypo-*) the ovary (*-gynous*). Opposite of epigynous.

I

imbibition: The process by which seeds absorb water.

imperfect flower: A flower lacking either male (stamens) or female (pistils) parts, or both. (4)

inarching: Grafting in which the scion and stock, each planted and bearing roots, are joined. The younger, scion plant may be used as support for the older or may be severed from its roots after the union has healed and treated as an addition to the older tree. (11)

incipient wilt: See wilting point.

incompatible: The condition wherein certain plants are not capable of interbreeding or of being grafted. (19)

incomplete flower: A flower that lacks one or more of the following parts: carpels, stamens, petals, sepals.

indicator plant: A plant that is characteristic of certain soil or site conditions. A plant that is sensitive to a certain disease and is therefore used in indexing. (3,4)

indehiscent: A fruit not opening along a suture or valve. (11)

indeterminate: A habit of plant growth wherein vegetative growth continues after the start of flowering and until the death of the plant.

index: To determine the presence or absence of a viral disease, usually by grafting the test plant to a sensitive indicator plant. (4)

indoleacetic acid: (IAA). A synthetic growth regulator in the auxin group. (11)

indolebutyric acid: (IBA). A synthetic growth regulator in the auxin group often used to stimulate rooting in cuttings. (11)

infiltration: The downward entry of surface water into soil. (3)

inferior ovary: An ovary appearing to be beneath the other flower parts. An epigynous flower has an inferior ovary. (11)

inflorescence: The arrangement of flowers on a floral axis. Also, a cluster of flowers. (4)

infructescence: The inflorescence in the fruiting state. (15)

inlay graft: A type of approach graft. A slot of bark about four inches long is removed from the stock and the tip of the scion plant, cut in a long tapering fashion, and fitted into the slot and tacked in place.

inoculate: To treat seed with microorganisms for a specific beneficial response. Usually refers to the treatment of legume seeds with *Rhizobium* to stimulate nitrogen fixation. (3)

inoculum: A pathogen which can cause infection. (4)

inorganic fertilizer: A fertilizer not having carbon as a basic component. (3)

insect: Any of a large group of small invertebrate animals. True insects, when adults, have three pairs of legs and three well-defined body regions.

insecticide: A chemical substance that kills insects. (17)

insolation: Solar radiation impinging upon the earth.

integrated pest management: (IPM). A system of pest control utilizing a combination of cultural, chemical, biological, and physical practices. (19)

intercalary: Meristematic tissue in areas other than the apical meristems. (19)

intercrop: Any crop planted between the rows of another for the purpose of double-cropping the land.

internode: The portion of the stem between the nodes. (4)

interstem: (interstock, stem builder). A short section of stem tissue grafted between the rootstock and the scion to improve compatibility, winter hardiness, etc.

involucre: A group of small leaves or bracts usually surrounding the head of a flower or fruit, as in the daisy and the female flower of the hickory. (10)

ion: An atom or bundle of atoms having an electric charge. (1)

iron sulfate: (ferrous sulfate, copperas crystals, green vitriol). A compound used to supply iron to the soil. Also, formerly used to destroy broad-leaved perennial weeds in lawns. (11)

irregular flower: A flower which has sepals and petals of different proportions.

J

joint: The node of a grass culm. (16)

June drop: The final shedding of fruit after bloom and before natural ripening. It usually occurs in late May or June in the Northern Hemisphere. The term is most often applied to apples. (9)

juno: A type of iris.

juvenile (plant): A plant that has not yet developed the ability to flower. (4)

K

keel: A ridged portion of a flower resembling the keel of a boat; commonly seen in the pea and sweet pea. (11)

kelp: A seaweed species once used extensively for fertilizer and as a source of potassium. Seaweed contains about 1% nitrogen, 0.5% phosphorus, and up to 14% potassium. (2)

kenrot: A physiological disorder of tulips wherein the entire stem above the top leaf dies. (9)

kieserite: See magnesium sulfate.

king flower: Usually, the first flower to open in a cluster. It is often the largest and produces the largest fruit.

kitchen garden: A garden that may produce vegetables, salad greens, herbs, and small fruit for the home table. (18)

knaur: See burl.

knee roots: Roots moving up aboveground as a result of soil waterlogging. (4)

kniffen system: A method of training grape vines to a support. The four-cane kniffen system employs two wires with two canes on each side of the trunk trained singly to each wire.

knot garden: A garden made with small hedges or bedding plants in elaborate designs resembling the patterns used in embroidery and tatting. (8)

knuckling: A condition in tulips, in which the shoot emerges bent over with the flower head still in the bulb. (9)

kremnophyte: A plant growing upon a wall or cliff. (8)

L

L: (St). In tomatoes, the disease resistance codes for grey leaf spot, or *Stemphyllium.*

laevigate: Smooth, polished. (15)

lambourd: A fruit spur.

lanceolate: Lance-shaped. (15)

land plaster: See calcium sulfate.

larva: The immature stage of many insects, exemplified by grubs, caterpillars, and maggots. (18)

latent bud: A bud that remains dormant the season after its production. (4)

latent heat of soil: The relatively constant temperature of the soil over an extended period of time. (19)

lateral: A side shoot or root.

lateral meristem: A meristem that produces secondary tissue and is responsible for an increase in stem diameter.

latewood: (summerwood). The denser portion of the annual xylem growth ring produced in summer. (14)

latex: The milky juice of some plants, such as milkweed and lettuce. (15)

lath house: An outdoor growing structure covered with lath spaced to allow about half the light to penetrate to the plants. (6)

laticifer: Latex-producing cell.

lawn: An area covered by short grass, usually kept mown. (18)

lawn substitute: A ground cover located in areas where grasses do not do well.

layby application: The application of a material such as lime or fertilizer with or after the last cultivation of the season. (14)

layering: A method of vegetative propagation. Shoots of the parent are bent down and pinned to the soil (simple layering); humus is placed on a wound in the stem (air layering); the mother plant is cut back and soil mounded around new, adventitious shoots (mound layering, or stooling); the burying and exposure of alternate areas of a long shoot or vine (serpentine layering). (8,9)

LD$_{50}$: The amount of a chemical that will kill 50% of the test population. It is usually expressed as milligrams per kilogram of body weight.

leaching: Removal of soluble salts by the downward movement of water through the soil. (1,3)

lead: New growth in orchids arising from the main dormant bud at the base of the old growth.

leader: The main shoot of a tree. (4)

leaf: A plant organ wherein food is manufactured in the presence of chlorophyll through photosynthesis. (18)

leaf bud: A bud producing only vegetative tissue. (4)

leaflet: A small leaf; part of a compound leaf.

leaf mold: Partially decomposed leaves meshed together with fungal mycelia and used as a soil amendment. (14)

leaf scar: The mark remaining on a shoot after leaf fall, denoting the former point of attachment. (15)

leaf stalk: Petiole.

leggy: Spindly. A condition usually caused by overfeeding or low light conditions.

legume: A cultivated plant of the Fabaceae (Leguminosae), a family containing beans, peas, alfalfa, and other plants. The family is important because of the bacteria living in nodules in the roots which can fix nitrogen. (8)

lemma: A bract of a spikelet above the glumes in grasses. (16)

lenticels: Small corky areas on the surfaces of stems, some fruit, and roots, that allow for the interchange of gases. (4)

lepage: A training system for fruit trees wherein scaffolds are trained into a series of arches.

liana: A woody vine. (8)

lichen: A group of plants that consist of fungi and algae living together in a symbiotic relationship. (8)

lift: To harvest rooted cuttings from the propagation bed. More broadly, the transplanting of plants from one place to another. (5,10)

light soil: A sandy, coarse textured soil, indicative of excellent drainage and aeration.

ligne: See line.

ligule: A thin portion of tissue where the leaf blade and sheath meet in the grasses. Also, the rather long, narrow corolla of the ray flowers in members of the composite family. (11)

limb: A branch. A free segment of a perianth. (12)

limbing out: Removing branches.

lime: (agricultural lime, limestone, ground lime). A material containing calcium and/or magnesium used to neutralize soil acidity. It contains about 44% calcium and 5% magnesium. The term can also apply to quicklime (burned lime, caustic lime, lump lime, and unslaked lime), which contains about 74% calcium and 9% magnesium, and to hydrated lime, which contains about 76% calcium, 9% magnesium, and 24% water. These materials have differing degrees of reactivity and neutralizing ability and are not interchangeable. For general home use, regular ground limestone is usually preferred. (1,2)

lime sulfur: This is used as a source of calcium and sulfur and as a fungicide. It contains about 6% calcium and 23% sulfur and can be phytotoxic. (2)

liming materials: In addition to standard lime, these can include other material containing calcium and/or magnesium that are used to neutralize soil acidity. Materials include marl and oyster shells. (1,2)

line: (line out, ligne). To transplant in a line; to arrange container plants in a line. A group of plants having the same ancestry and propagated by seed. A cultivar propagated by seed. Also, a twelfth of an inch, a measurement used in botanical descriptions and now obsolete. Also spelled ligne. (8)

liner: A young plant lined out closely in rows. (9)

linseed meal: The dried, ground product of pressed flaxseed meal. It contains about 5% nitrogen, 2% phosphorus, 1.3% potassium, and 85% organic matter. It can be used as a fertilizer in home gardens. (2)

lip: The portion of an irregular corolla that resembles a protruding lip, as in snapdragons, the mints, figworts, and many orchids. (10)

LISA: The acronym for Low-Input Sustainable Agriculture. (17)

litter: Partially decomposed leaves, straw, etc., accumulated on the soil surface beneath trees or other vegetation. (8)

liverwort: A group of plants with no true roots and odd, leaflike structures. They are found in damp soil, moss, or on damp rocks. (8)

loam: A textural class of soil containing sand, silt, and clay. (3)

locule: A chamber in an ovary, anther, or fruit. (4)

lodging: The condition wherein plants, usually the cereal grains, bend near the soil line and eventually fall. (14)

loggia: An expansive, pretentious outdoor sitting room enclosed on one side and with the roof supported by columns on the other. (11)

long-day plant: A plant which can flower only after receiving light for a period longer than a certain "critical photoperiod," usually ranging from 11 to 14 hours. (4)

lorette: A system of pruning in which the leaders are tipped in the spring and the laterals pruned nearly to their bases during the summer. (13)

lump lime: See lime.

M

macronutrient: A nutrient used in relatively large quantities by the plant. It usually refers to nitrogen, phosphorus, potassium, calcium, and magnesium. (3)

magnesium sulfate: (epsom salts, kieserite). This compound is used to supply magnesium to plants where alteration of the soil pH through the use of dolomitic lime is undesirable. The material may be used alone or mixed with fertilizers. It contains about 17% magnesium. (1,2)

maiden tree: A tree having one year's growth above the graft. (13)

malling: A series of size-controlling apple rootstocks developed at the East Malling Research Station in England.

manure: The excrement of animals, together with straw or other bedding. The average analysis (N,P,K) of various manures is as follows: Horse: 0.7-.25-.5; Cattle: 0.6-0.15-0.45; Swine: 0.5-0.35-0.4; Sheep: 0.95-0.35-1.0; Chicken: 1.0-0.8-0.4; Goat: 1.5-1.3-3.0. True composition depends upon animal species, feed, bedding, and how the manure was stored. Much of all manure is made up of humus. (1,2)

manure tea: The suspension of manure in water, which is then strained and applied to plants to enhance growth.

marchand: A training system wherein whips are planted at a 45-degree angle to the ground, facing north, and the shoots are trained at right angles to the trunk.

market garden: A commercial farm near a large metropolitan area where vegetables are grown. (11)

marl: Soft earth deposits containing about 42% calcium in the form of calcium carbonate. It is used in place of ground limestone to neutralize soil acidity. (1,2)

mass planting: A closely spaced arrangement of plants.

mat: A covering of straw or fabric, for hotbeds and coldframes, to protect the plants against injurious cold. (7)

MDM: In corn, the disease resistance code for maize dwarf mosaic.

meadow peat: See muck.

mealybug: A small insect that attacks plants. It is usually covered with a white waxy material that resembles a bit of cotton.

medium: The material in or on which plants are grown. *pl.* media. (9)

meiosis: Reduction cell division wherein the number of chromosomes is halved.

meristem: A region of tissue containing mitotic cell division, such as in the cambium and at the apex of roots and shoots. (4)

mesocarp: The center of a fruit wall; the edible flesh of cherry, peach, and plum. (19)

mesophyte: A plant that grows in soil with moderate amounts of moisture; intermediate between the hydrophytes and the xerophytes.

metered-release fertilizer: See controlled-release fertilizer.

microclimate: The climate of a small area resulting from the modification of the overall climate due to changes in wind and sun exposure and in elevation. (3)

microfauna: Microscopic animals such as nematodes and protozoa. (3)

microflora: Microscopic plants such as bacteria, fungi, and algae. (3)

micronutrient: See minor element.

micropropagation: (tissue culture). Production from very small plant parts grown in a test tube wherein the environment is completely controlled. (4)

midrib: The central vein of a leaf.

mignon: In dahlias, a single with plants up to 18 inches in height.

mil: A measurement for the thickness of plastic covering material. One mil equals 1/1000 inch.

millerandage: The condition in grapes where the seeds remain abnormally small and the berry does not size. (9)

milorganite: An organic fertilizer manufactured by the Sewerage Commission of Milwaukee, Wisconsin containing about 6% nitrogen and 4% total phosphoric acid. (1)

minor element: (micronutrient, trace element). Essential nutrients used by the plant in small amounts. These include boron, clorine, copper, iron, manganese, molybdenum, and zinc. (1,3)

miscible oils: Vegetable or mineral oils easily emulsifiable in water and used as an insecticide. (11)

misting: Spraying plant foliage with water to remove dust and to increase humidity.

mite: A small creature commonly referred to as an insect but actually belonging to the spider group. It has four pairs of legs instead of the three common to insects.

miticide: A chemical substance that kills mites. (17)

mitosis: Cell division wherein the number of chromosomes is first doubled, then halved.

mixed bud: A bud containing both flower and vegetative parts.

mixed fertilizer: Two or more fertilizer materials blended together.

modified central leader: In fruit trees, when the central leader is tipped back to a side branch to control plant height.

monocarp: A plant that remains vegetative for a number of years, flowers once, and then dies.

monocotyledon: (monocot). A class of flowering plants having a single cotyledon. (14)

monoculture: A cultural practice wherein the same species is grown on the same ground for a number of years or where a single species is grown on a large acreage.

monoecious: The condition of having both male and female flower parts on different flowers of the same plant, as in corn.

morphology: The study of the whole form of an organism.

mosaic: A virus disease that causes the foliage to become mottled with light green or yellow over dark green. (17)

moss: A group of simple plants found on damp soils, the bark of trees, rocks, and in bogs. They have a large capacity to hold water. (8)

mother bulb: The old bulb around which bulblets form. (10)

mother plant: (mother block). See stock plant.

mounding: (mound layering). See layering.

MTO: In lettuce, the code for *mosaic tested* to *0* in 30,000 seeds. That is, there is no incidence of mosaic virus in that number of seeds.

muck: (meadow peat, swamp muck). Organic soil wherein the original organic materials are unrecognizable. It is often darker and contains more minerals than peat. (3)

mucronate: Tipped with a short, abruptly tapered point. (15)

mudding: See puddling.

mulch: Any material, organic or inorganic, that is spread on top of the soil to protect the plant and its roots from desiccation, erosion, temperature extremes, frost heaving, soil crusting, etc. (3)

mull: A layer of decomposed organic matter and some mineral soil between the top of the A-horizon and the bottom of the duff. (8)

multiple superphosphate: See double superphosphate.

mum: An abbreviation for chrysanthemum. (5)

muriate: An alternate word for chloride.

muriate of potash: (potassium chloride). This fertilizer material usually contains 80% potassium chloride, which yields about 50% potash. The 90 to 99% potassium chloride yields about 60% potash. (1)

mushroom soil (spent): Usually, well-rotted horse manure once used to grow mushrooms but deemed no longer satisfactory. It contains about 1% nitrogen, 1% phosphorus, 0.8% potassium and 28% organic matter. (2)

must: Crushed fruit and juice. (4)

mutation: An abrupt change in heredity, caused by a change in a gene, producing new individuals differing from their parents. (18)

mycelia: The threadlike bodies of some fungi which appear on the surfaces of some roots and in the soil. *sing* Mycelium. (8)

mycorrhiza: Usually, the symbiotic association of a specific fungus with the roots of higher plants. (3)

N

N: In tomatoes, the code for indicating resistance to nematodes.

nastic movement: The movement of a plant or plant part that is not caused by external stimuli, such as in the helical twining movement of pea vines.

NCLB: In corn, the disease resistance code for northern corn leaf blight.

neck: The thickened upper portion of some bulbs and tuberous roots, such as onion and rutabaga. (10)

necrosis: Dead, decaying tissue.

nectar: A sugary liquid excreted by glands at the base of some flowers.

nectary: A gland or other structure that secretes nectar. (4)

nematocide: A chemical substance that kills nematodes.

nematode: Microscopic, nonsegmented roundworms that often cause or transmit diseases. (4)

net venation: (reticulate venation). The arrangement of veins within a leaf that resembles a net. (19)

neutral soil: A soil that is neither acid nor alkaline, having a pH of seven. (18)

nitrate: Nitrogen combined with oxygen as NO_3. (1)

nitrate of potash: See potassium nitrate.

nitrate of soda: (sodium nitrate). A fertilizer containing about 16% nitrate nitrogen. (1)

nitrate of soda-potash: A fertilizer containing nitrates of sodium and potassium, with at least 14% nitrogen and 14% potash. (1)

nitrification: The formation of nitrate or nitrite compounds from ammonia. The process proceeds rapidly in warm, moist, neutral soils and ceases when soil temperatures fall below 40°F. (1,2)

nitrite: Nitrogen combined with oxygen as NO_2.

nitrogen fixation: The chemical combining of free nitrogen by bacteria in the roots of legumes. (1)

node: The point of attachment of a leaf to a shoot. (4)

nodule: (tubercle). A pealike swelling on the roots of legumes, containing bacteria that are involved in nitrogen fixation.

nodule bacteria: The bacteria that fix nitrogen, found within nodules on the roots, stem, or leaves of certain plants, usually legumes. (3)

normal sugary: (Su). Sweet corn cultivars containing the Su gene that allows for the normal development of sugar which is rapidly converted to starch after harvest.

normal superphosphate: (superphosphate). A product of the treatment of phosphate rock with sulfuric acid. It is used as a fertilizer and contains 16 to 20% available phosphoric acid. (1)

notch: To make a shallow nick above a young bud to force development of vegetative growth or just below a bud to force development of reproductive growth. (9)

no-till: (stubble culture). The practice of planting seeds in a field from which the former crop was removed or killed with herbicides, without first tilling the soil. (14)

noxious weed: A plant legally classed as being especially trouble-some. (9)

NPK: The common abbreviations for Nitrogen, Phosphorus, and Potassium (Greek = Kalium).

nurse crop: A crop sown with another crop that will emerge before the second, break the soil crust, and mark the row. An example would be the fast-emerging radish sown with the slow-emerging parsnip.

nut: A dry, indehiscent fruit with a husk covering a hardened shell.

O

oedema: Small, nonpathogenic corky spots on the undersides of leaves, usually of *Geranium,* that are caused by longtime exposure of the plant to excessive moisture. (15)

offset: A lateral shoot arising near the base of a plant and rooting at its tip, thus producing a daughter plant. Similar to a stolon and runner, it is commonly found in the crinums, agaves, and the house-leek. (10)

offshoot: A short, often horizontal shoot arising near the crown of a plant. (19)

olericulture: The production of vegetables. (17)

onion hoe: A small implement with a narrow blade used to weed between small seedlings.

onocyclus: A group of irises that have a single flower to a spathe, and hairs on the falls. (15)

open-pollination: Free exchange of pollen without regard to culti-var. (4)

organic: A material or compound composed mostly of carbon. The compound may be either natural or synthetic. (1,2)

organic fertilizer: A fertilizer composed chiefly of organic materi-als, such as manure and compost. It may also contain mineral nutri-ents in a non-processed form, such as rock phosphate.

organic soil: Soils high in organic matter, often containing 80% or more soil. (1,4)

ornamental: A plant grown for the beauty of its form, foliage, flowers or fruit rather than for food, fiber, or to meet some other useful purpose. (18)

osmoconditioning: (priming). Treating seeds with water to speed metabolism and germination. The process does not proceed to radicle emergence. (17)

osmosis: The diffusion of a solution across semipermiable cell membranes.

osmunda fiber: The roots of the osmunda fern often used for potting orchids. (18)

ovary: The swollen base of the pistil containing the ovules. Upon fertilization, the ovary develops into the fruit. (17)

overcolor: The pigmentation of a flower or fruit that develops over the ground color as the plant matures. For example, red is the overcolor of a 'McIntosh' apple that develops over the green ground color.

overpotting: Growing plants in pots that are excessively large. (10)

ovicide: A chemical substance that kills mite eggs. (17)

ovule: The portions of the ovary that contain the eggs and which, following fertilization, become the seeds. (10)

oyster shell: Ground oyster shells used as limestone to neutralize soil acidity. The material contains about 47% calcium. (2)

P

palea: The inner bract of a grass floret. (16)

palmate leaf: A compound leaf having all leaflets arising from a single place at the tip of the petiole. (19)

pan: A layer of soil that is highly compacted. A shallow dishlike object similar to a flower pot but with shorter sides than those of a pot, used to hold or start plants and bulbs. They are usually two to six inches deep and six to eight inches wide. (8,11)

panicle: A long, compound, loose inflorescence.

pannose: Covered with a thick coating of woolly hair. (15)

pappus: The tuft of hair on some seeds and fruit.

parallel venation: A system of leaf venation wherein the major veins run parallel along the blade.

parasite: An organism that lives on or in another organism or plant, to the detriment of the host plant. (18)

parterre: A garden area containing ornamental beds separated by paths in a formal setting. The paths may contain colored gravel, stone or small plants to add color. Also, a similar arrangement with lawns and pools. (11)

parthenocarpy: Fruit set, either natural or induced, without fertilization. (4)

partnership cropping: Growing two crops simultaneously with the same season of maturity and the same growing season length but with different habits. An example would be planting winter squash with corn. (11)

pathogen: A disease-causing organism.

peanut hull meal: Ground peanut hulls sometimes mixed with fertilizers as a filler. It contains about 1% nitrogen, 0.2% phosphorus, 0.8% potash and 88% organic matter. (2)

peat: Partially decomposed plant residues that have accumulated in an anaerobic environment, usually under water. Although peat contains some nutrients, its primary value is in supplying a weed-free organic material with high water-holding capacity. Reed-sedge peat (pH = 6.3) can hold about 6.5 times its weight in moisture, acid peat and sphagnum moss (pH about five) can hold up to 20 times their weight in moisture. (2,8)

peat moss: Commonly, the dried, shredded peat from sphagnum moss. (10)

peat pot: A pot made of pressed peat moss used for starting young plants. (18)

pedicel: The flower or fruit stalk of an inflorescence.

peduncle: The stalk of the flower cluster. (15)

pelletized seed: Seed coated with a uniform layer of clay, with or without fertilizer, to aid in proper plant spacings and in more rapid emergence. Usually used with very small or irregularly shaped seed. (9)

peltate: Shield-shaped. (15)

pepo: A modified berry with a hard rind composed of the receptacle and the exocarp tissue, as in muskmelon.

perennial: Surviving for many years. A woody perennial, such as an oak tree, increases in size each year. The aboveground portions of an herbaceous perennial may die back each autumn in colder climates.

perfect flower: Having both male and female parts. (4,11)

perianth: The floral envelope as a whole. A collective term for the calyx and corolla. (4,11)

pericarp: The wall of a ripened ovary encompassing the epicarp, mesocarp, and endocarp.

pericycle: A tissue in roots from which branch roots arise.

perigynous: A type of flower wherein the receptacle envelopes a portion of the ovary.

perlite: A volcanic glass puffed under tremendous heat. It contains about 4% potassium and is used chiefly as a lightweight amendment to increase soil porosity. (2)

permaculture: The use of edible plants in the home landscape. (9)

permanent wilting point: See wilting point.

perpetual: A flower type which continues to bloom as long as growth continues, as in perpetual carnations, perpetual roses, etc. (11)

pesticide: A general term that describes a material used to control any sort of pest. (17)

petal: One of the separate, modified, and often colored leaves of a corolla, within the calyx of a flower. (18)

petiole: A leaf stalk. (5)

petiolule: Stalk of a leaflet.

pH: A term indicating the degree of acidity or alkalinity of a material. A pH of seven is neutral, while values above seven are alkaline and those below seven, acid. The values are expressed on a logarithmic scale from 0 to 14. Therefore, each value differs from the one below or above it by a factor of ten. For example, a pH of five is ten times more acid than one of six and 100 times more acid than one of seven. (1,2)

phenotype: The outside appearance of a plant. (17)

pheromone: Chemical substances excreted by an insect or animal that can produce a given response in another of the same species. (9)

phloem: The major food conducting tissue of a plant, located just outside the cambium. (4)

phosphate rock: A material composed mostly of tricalcium phosphate. It contains about 32% phosphorus and, if finely ground, can be used as a slowly available source of phosphorus. (1,2)

photodegradable: Broken down by sunlight.

photoperiodism: Flowering in response to the length of day (or, more properly, night). (15)

photosynthesis: The process by which sugars are made from water and carbon dioxide in the chloroplasts in the presence of light. (8)

phototropism: The bending of plants toward light. (8)

phyllotaxy: The arrangement of leaves around a stem. (19)

phylloxera: A small insect that attacks the roots and leaves of grapes. (4)

picotee: (piquettes, piquettees). A variety of carnation and petunia, having petals bordered with a color other than the primary flower color. (11)

pinch: (stop). To remove the tip of a stem, usually by pinching between the thumb and forefinger. (5)

pin-eyed: A tubular flower wherein the stigmas are visible in the throat but the stamens are not. The opposite of thrum-eyed. (10)

pink: Plants of the genus *Dianthus,* but also commonly used to refer to those of the related genera *Silene* and *Lychnis* and certain other genera. (10)

pinnate: Having the form of a feather. (15)

pip: The small dormant crown or other propagative portion of the lily of the valley, peony, and anemone, consisting of a bud and roots arising from the rootstock. A seed of the "pip-fruits" (apple, pear, quince, etc.). A synonym for apple cultivars called "pippins." A segment of the surface of the pineapple. A single flower of the *Auricula. (*10,11)

piping: An old term for layering.

pistil: The female portion of the flower, composed of the stigma, style, and ovary. (4)

pistillate flower: A female flower. (4)

pith: The spongy tissue at the center of young stems and roots. (4)

pit house: A large, sunken cold frame. (15)

plant nutrients: The nutrients essential for the proper growth of most plants: oxygen, carbon, hydrogen, nitrogen, potassium, calcium, sulfur, phosphorus, magnesium, manganese, iron, zinc, boron, copper, molybdenum, chlorine. Some plants also require nickel and vanadium in trace amounts. (2)

pleach: (plash). To prune and train trees by interweaving the branches to form a single hedge or archway. (10)

plicata: Irises that are stippled with dark over light ground color. (12)

plow layer: The surface layer, usually eight or nine inches, of soil turned in normal tilling operations.

plow pan: (plow sole). A firm, impermeable layer of soil formed from continuous plowing at the same depth.

plug: A small rooted cutting grown in a triangular or square hole in a plastic tray. The tight rootball formed eliminates the need for peat pots.

plugging: Establishment of a new lawn by inserting small cones, or plugs, of sod into the soil.

plumule: The growing point of an embryo. (17)

plunge: To bury a pot, in which a plant is growing, up to its rim in soil or growing media. (10)

PM: In melons and cucumbers, the disease resistance code for powdery mildew.

pod: A dry, dehiscent fruit. (15)

pogoniris: Irises having beards. (12)

pollard: A tree whose main branches have been cut back to the trunk to form a head of many dense branches. (8)

pollen: Small, usually yellow, grains released from the anthers that carry the male gametes for fertilization.

pollen tube: The tubular projection from a germinated pollen grain through which sperm pass to the female gametophyte.

pollinate: The transfer of pollen from anther to stigma. (4)

pollinator: The causative agent of pollination, such as wind, bees, etc. (4)

pollinizer: The pollen producer. (4)

polyantha: A type of rose that produces small flowers intermittently on small plants.

polyethylene: A clear plastic material used as a covering for greenhouses. Black polyethylene is often used as a mulch in gardens.

pome: A fruit from a species belonging to the subfamily Pomoideae, of the family Rosaceae, i.e., apple, pear, quince, hawthorn, and medlar. (9)

pomology: The study of fruit. (8)

pompon: Small, compact, buttonlike heads of flowers, usually of chrysanthemums and dahlias. (10)

pore space: The space between the soil particles, typically about 50% of the soil volume.

postemergence: Applied after the emergence of a weed or crop. (9)

potash: (potassium oxide). The potassium content of fertilizers is given as potash. (1)

potassium chloride: A salt of potash containing at least 48% potassium. (1)

potassium nitrate: (saltpeter, nitrate of potash). A potassium salt of nitric acid containing about 13% nitrogen and 44% potash. (1)

potassium sulfate: (sulfate of potash). A low chloride potassium salt of sulfuric acid containing about 48% potassium. (1)

potbound: (root bound). The stage of growth of a potted plant when the roots completely fill the container and become a solid, fibrous mass unable to grow freely. (7)

potting mix: See also soil mix. A medium for potting plants. There are several specialized mixes.

potting on: Transplanting plants from seedlings to maturity in successively larger pots, moving to the next larger size as soon as the roots have filled the pot. (7)

potting up: Transplanting plants from seedling flats or trays to flower pots, or from outdoors into pots for overwintering. (7)

preemergence: Applied before the emergence of a certain weed or crop plant. (9)

prickle: A thornlike or hairlike growth on a plant formed from the bark. Roses have prickles, not thorns. (8)

prick-off: (prick-out). To transplant seedlings from flat to pot or to another flat. (5)

prill: A small, spherical pellet formed when molten material is sprayed through cool air. (2)

primary flower: The flower that terminates the central axis of a cluster, as in the strawberry. It usually blooms first and produces the largest fruit. (4)

primary plant food: Nitrogen, phosphorus, and potassium. (1,2)

priming: See osmoconditioning.

primocane: The vegetative first year cane of a bramble, such as in the raspberry. (4)

process tankage: A dark brown fluffy material containing about eight percent nitrogen. It is made by processing animal waste products, such as feathers and leather scraps, under pressure. (2)

procumbent: Lying on the ground without rooting. (4)

proliferous: Having buds or bulblets in the inflorescence. (16)

propagation: The production of new plants from parent stock. (18)

prop root: A root that acts as support, as in corn. (10)

prostrate: See procumbent.

pruning: The removal of dead, injured, or unnecessary wood from woody plants. (8)

pruning hook: See bramble hook.

pseudobulb: The spherical, fleshy, hard stem in orchids adapted for water storage.

puddling: (mudding). The process of coating the roots with a fine mud before planting to reduce drying. Also said of heavy soils that are worked when wet, making them become hard and impermeable when dried. (10,11)

pulse: Legume; beans and peas. (9)

pulvinus: A swelling at the base of the branches of some grass panicles and the leaves of certain plants which cause them to spread apart. (16)

pumice: Siliceous, volcanic rock which is light and porous. It is often used as an abrasive. (8)

pup: The offshoot of a bromeliad which can be easily removed from the parent and grown on its own. Also, any small plant formed on stems or roots.

PVY: In peppers, the disease resistance code for potato virus Y.

pyriform: Pear-shaped. (16)

Q

quick: A term used to describe land in good tilth.

quicklime: See calcium oxide and lime.

quiescence: Dormancy controlled by external environmental factors. (4)

quincunx: A planting pattern in which four plants are set at the corners of a square and a fifth is set in the middle of the square.

R

raceme: A type of inflorescence in which the spikelets are composed of several pedicels on a rachis. (16)

rachis: The axis of a spike or raceme. (16)

radicle: The initial, young root emerging from a seed.

raffia: Dried fibers from the cuticle of the Madagascar palm fashioned into small rope or string and used for various gardening purposes. It usually rots after a season in the field. (11)

rake: A garden implement with teeth or tines mounted on a long handle and used for gathering leaves, grass clippings, etc., or for smoothing the soil. The hang of a roof beyond the endwalls.

raphe: The seamlike union of two halves of an organ, often marked with a ridge or furrow. (15)

ratoon: A sucker used for propagation in pineapple, sugarcane, banana, and other plants. (10)

rattan: A genus of palm. Also, sections of palm stems made into wicker furniture. (9)

rayflower: Any one of many small flowers forming a ring around the disk flowers of a composite head.

reaction, soil: The pH of the soil. (3)

reaction wood: Wood formed in the portions of trees and limbs that lean or are not in an upright position. The compression wood of conifers and the tension wood of deciduous plants. (19)

receptacle: In fruit, the enlarged end of a pedicel to which one or more flowers are attached. It may become the edible portion of a mature fruit, as in the strawberry, or embedded in it, as in the apple.

reed-stemmed: A type of orchid that has tall, stiff, strong stems only a few millimeters in diameter.

refoliate: To produce new leaves after having lost the old leaves.

rejuvenate: To renew the health and vigor of a plant by pruning, fertilizing, or repotting. (18)

remontant: Possessing a second season of bloom, as in some roses and delphiniums. (10)

renovate: To cut back severely and/or narrow plant rows to rejuvenate a planting. Often done in strawberries and asparagus. Rows are narrowed by removing plants that have spread into the aisles.

rest: Dormancy controlled by internal factors usually requiring a chilling period for release. (4)

reticulata: A type of iris.

reticulate: Netlike. Forming a network. (15)

retrorse: Pointing backwards. (16)

rhizome: Rootlike, underground stem giving rise to roots below and shoots above. (4)

rhizosphere: The soil immediately near the root. (8)

rib: A vein in a leaf. Also, the five carpel lines visible on the surface of an apple or other fruit of the rose family.

ridge: See blanch.

ridging hoe: An implement with a broad blade used for mounding soil around plants.

rill: Furrow.

ringing: Removing a thin strip of bark around a trunk or branch, usually to induce the formation of flower buds.

ripeness to flower: The minimum vegetative size and physiologic age a plant must attain before it can flower.

rock garden: A garden for the culture of small, alpine plants. (11)

rogue: As a verb, the removal of diseased or otherwise undesirable individuals from a population. As a noun, an off-type or diseased plant. (4,17)

roll: To move a heavy roller over a lawn area in the spring to smooth out frost heaves, or as a preplanting practice to smooth the soil.

root: A part of a plant, usually underground, the main functions of which are to anchor the plant, and absorb moisture and nutrients. (18)

rootball: The mass of roots and the soil attached to them that is removed from the ground or container during transplanting. (19)

root bound: See potbound.

root cap: The mass of cells protecting the root apical meristem.

root crop: A plant grown for its edible root, such as carrots, beets, and turnips. Potatoes are sometimes included here, though their edible portion is a stem tuber. (9)

root crown: The part of the plant where the root and the shoot system meet. (17)

root hair: A single-celled extension on a root which absorbs water and nutrients.

rooting hormone: A substance applied to plant tissue to stimulate the production of roots. (18)

rooting medium: A material into which cuttings are placed to help induce their rooting. (18)

root knee: A large projection from a horizontal root. (9)

root nodule: A swelling on the root, usually in legumes, as a result of invasion by nitrogen fixing bacteria.

root pressure: The fluid pressure in the roots that may aid in the movement of liquid up the plant axis and which is responsible for guttation and bleeding.

root pruning: Cutting off the roots completely around and some distance out from the plant to lessen transplant shock, induce dwarfing, or increase return bloom.

rootstock: See stock.

root tuber: A thickened portion of a root responsible for the storage of carbohydrates. (19)

root zone: The volume of soil containing the plant roots. (19)

rosarium: Obsolete name for a rose garden. (10)

rose-nozzle: A fan-shaped or circular nozzle that can be attached to a watering can, hose, etc., for sprinkling.

rosette: A cluster of basal leaves, as in dandelion, common in the first year of a biennial plant's cycle. Also, the condition of having leaves in a small, tight, radiating cluster.

rotation: (rotation cropping). A planned sequence of crops growing in a regular succession on the same land. (3)

row cover: A lightweight material, usually plastic or polyester, used to cover the entire row of plants as early season protection against frost and cool temperatures.

Rt: In corn, the disease resistance code for rust.

rugose: Wrinkled. (16)

runnel: A pollarded tree. (10)

runner: See stolon.

rust: A fungal disease that requires two separate host plants for the completion of its life cycle. (19)

S

salad crop: A plant grown for its leaves and which is usually eaten fresh. Plants in this group include lettuce, endive, parsley, and cress. (9)

saline soil: A nonalkali soil that contains sufficient quantities of soluble salts to interfere with plant growth. (1)

salt hay: Hay cut from salt marshes, especially valuable for mulching. (11)

salt index: A way to express the comparative burning of plants caused by certain salts. The burning is caused by the salts' increasing the osmotic pressure of the soil solution. It is generally better to avoid fertilizers with high salt indices unless sufficient water will be available. (2)

saltpeter: See potassium nitrate.

samara: An indehiscent fruit wherein the pericarp forms wings, as in maples.

sand: A soil particle measuring between 0.05 and 2.0 millimeters in diameter. (3)

sap: The watery, circulating fluid in plants. (18)

saprophyte: A plant that lives on decaying organic matter. (8)

sapwood: The outer portion of the xylem where active conduction of water takes place. (4)

savoy: The natural crinkling of the leaf surface, usually in cabbage and spinach.

Sb: In cucumbers, the disease resistance code for scab.

scab: A disease, caused by a fungus, producing warty lesions on the fruit and leaves of peach, apple, pear, citrus, potato, *Gladiolus,* violet, and pansy. (15)

scabrous: Rough. (16)

scaffold branch: A main branch of a tree. A primary scaffold arising from the trunk.

scale: An insect pest having a waxy, shell-like covering. A modified leaf that protects a structure, as in a bud scale.

scandigie: A dibble, inserted at a right angle to the handle, formerly used for transplanting lettuce.

scape: A leafless flower stalk arising from the ground, as in the tulip and bloodroot. (10)

scarification: Loosening the soil without turning it. Scratching the coat of hard seeds to speed germination. (7)

schizocarp: An indehiscent fruit wherein the fruit divides into two or more indehiscent parts.

scion: (cion). The shoot section taken from a plant being propagated, containing one or more dormant buds. The top part of a graft. (4)

SCLB: In corn, the disease resistance code for southern corn leaf blight.

scooping: Procedure whereby a bulb's basal plate is removed and bulblets form at the base of the bulb scales.

scorch: Leaf injury caused by a lack of water, excessive transpiration, etc. (15)

scoring: Making an incision through the bark and completely around a trunk or branch to promote flowering. No bark is removed.

scree: The rocky surface of a mountain slope which spreads downward in a fan-shaped manner. (11)

screening plant: A plant used to cover the view or to separate areas of the landscape. (19)

Se: See Sugary enhanced.

Se+: See sugary enhanced+.

secondary flower: A flower that terminates the two main branches of the central floral axis, as in the strawberry. (4)

secondary plant food: Calcium, magnesium, and sulfur. (1,2)

secund: One-sided, or arranged along one side only. (16)

seed: The mature ovule of a flowering plant. (18)

seed tape: Seeds properly spaced and embedded on water-soluble plastic for easy planting. (9)

segment: One of the natural divisions in a flower. An iris has six segments. (12)

selective herbicide: An herbicide that kills only certain plants.

self-compatible: (-fruitful, -fertile, -setting). Capable of reproducing sexually by itself, without pollen from a plant of a different cultivar. (4)

self-pollination: The transfer of pollen from anther to stigma of the same flower or between flowers of the same cultivar. (4)

selfs: In carnations, the flowers of a single, solid color. (11)

self-sterile: A plant not able to be fertilized by its own pollen.

semi-determinate: Possessing a growth pattern with both determinate and indeterminate characteristics. (17)

semidwarf: A fruit tree that attains a height intermediate between a dwarf and a standard tree.

senescence: Old.

sepal: An outermost, often leaflike, nonsexual portion of a flower. (4)

separation: The use of the naturally detachable parts for propagation in bulbs and corms. (19)

sequestering agent: See chelate.

serpentine layering: See layering.

serrate: Saw-toothed. (16)

sessile: A leaf or other structure attached by its base, without a stalk.

set: A young transplant. A small bulb, such as an onion, used for transplanting. A sweet potato slip. Also, as a verb, it refers to a young, fertilized ovule in an ovary that has begun to develop into a fruit, in the sense of "The fruit has set."(11)

Sh$_2$: See supersweet.

shade house: A structure covered with lath or netting for the growth of shade-loving plants. (19)

shale: Fine-grained rock composed of silt and clay and formed under great pressure. (8)

shatter: Loss of aborted grape berries in the field or after harvest. Premature loss of snapdragon flowers because of poor pollination or environment. (4,9)

sheath: A tubular organ surrounding the base of a stalk, as in the grasses. (10)

sheugh: An obsolete term for heeling. (10)

shift: To transfer plants from pot to pot, usually while potting up. (11)

shock: The wilting or leaf abscission following the loss of a portion of the root system during transplanting, drought, or flooding. (19)

shoot: A side branch or new growth from the root of a plant. (18)

short-day plant: A plant that can flower only after receiving less than a "critical photoperiod," usually from eight to ten hours. (4)

shot berry: A very small, seedless, undeveloped grape. (4)

shrub: A woody plant that usually has multiple stems arising from the ground and is smaller than a tree. (8)

shuck: The outer husk of a fruit, as in hickory or corn. (10)

side-dress: To apply fertilizer or manure to a crop after emergence. It is applied between the rows or around each plant.

side graft: There are numerous types of side grafts, but all employ the technique of inserting the scion into the side of the stock.

signal: (signal patch). The splash of color on the hafts of the falls of some irises. (12)

silique: A slender, podlike dehiscent fruit, as those of the crucifer family. (17)

silk: The styles of the female flower of corn. Also, the stage at which these appear. The term "half-silk" refers to the stage in which about half the ears are in silk.

silt: A soil particle finer than sand but coarser than clay, between 0.05 and 0.002 millimeters in diameter. (3,8)

simple fruit: Fruit developed from a simple or compound pistil having no other parts. (4)

simple layering: See layering.

single: A dahlia with open centered flowers and only one row of ray flowers. (11)

sinus: A recess between two lobes of a leaf, as in the oak and grape. (10)

slab: A vining plant grown in containers and trained up a flat slab of wood.

slab-side: A carnation flower whose petals elongate on one side of the flower faster than on the other side, resulting in a lopsided flower. (9)

slate: Dense, fine-grained rock resulting from shale that was formed under heat and pressure. (8)

slat shed: See lath house. An outdoor growing structure covered with slats spaced so as to allow about half the light to penetrate to the plants. (6)

sleeve: A paper or plastic cone placed around a plant for protection during shipment. (5)

slime flux: The nonhardening, fluid outflow from the bark of many deciduous trees such as elm and maple, often, but not always, the result of wounding. (11)

slip: A cutting, especially from the sweet potato. A reference to the stage of ripeness in melons. The "half-slip" stage is reached when the stem has partially detached from the melon fruit; "full-slip" stage is reached when it is completely detached.

slipping: The time when the carnation inflorescence emerges from the leaf sheath.

slow-acting fertilizer: See controlled-release fertilizer.

slow-release fertilizer: See controlled-release fertilizer.

sludge: Solid, insoluble mixed mineral and organic material with variable composition that remains after treating sewage. It contains about 5% nitrogen, 4% phosphorus, 0.5% potassium, and 60% organic matter. (2,8)

slurry: A watery mixture.

small fruit: Fruit grown on small plants, such as raspberry, blackberry, blueberry, strawberry, cranberry, currant, and gooseberry. (9)

smother crop: A crop planted thickly to smother out undesirable weeds. Buckwheat is a good smother crop. (10)

smut: A fungus producing large masses of black spores, commonly found on corn, onion, and turfgrass. (15)

snag: The projecting base of a limb that remains on the plant after the limb has been cut off. (13)

snake spit: See frog spittle.

sobole: A sucker, especially one that develops into a tree as important as the main one. This condition is common in some palms. (10)

sod: A thick, one- to three-inch mat of plants, mostly grasses. (8)

sodic soil: See alkali soil.

sodium nitrate: See nitrate of soda.

softwood: The wood of conifers, which may not be soft.

soil: The life-sustaining surface of the earth, composed of disintegrated rock and some organic matter. (18)

soil aeration: See aeration, soil.

soil amendment: (soil conditioner). Substances used to change the acidity of a soil or its texture and water-holding capacity. They may not always have fertilizing value. Such materials include limestone, perlite, peat, slag, sand, and aluminum sulfate. Strictly, substances used to alter the pH are termed amendments and those used to alter texture, conditioners. (2)

soil cement: A water-resistant, hard surface made by mixing cement with the top two to four inches of mineral soil, then adding water by sprinkling. Sometimes used as a lining for pools, canals, and footpaths. It will not perform well on soils with high organic matter content, on slopes greater than 30%, or where it is subjected to much traffic. (8)

soil drench: A liquid, often a pesticide, poured over the root zone. (19)

soiless gardening: See hydroponics.

soil map: A map showing the location of different soils in an area and indicating their suitability for agricultural uses. (8)

soil mix: A mixture of several ingredients, such as sand, peat, and compost, used to create an artificial growing medium. (9)

soil solution: The soluble materials in a soil held in solution. (8)

soil structure: Arrangement of individual soil particles.

soil testing: The analysis of soil for the quantities of plant nutrients it contains. (18)

soil texture: The proportion of particles of various sizes (sand, silt, and clay) in a soil. (1)

soil type: The total of primary physical constituents of a soil, such as silty clay loam, fine sandy loam, sandy loam, loamy sand, etc. (1)

solanaceous crops: Plants in the family Solanaceae or nightshade family, grown for their edible fruit, such as the tomato, pepper, and eggplant. (9)

soluble fertilizer: A high analysis complete fertilizer, such as 20-20-20 with or without micronutrients. (9)

soluble salts: The total supply of soil minerals in solution. Some of these may be injurious. (5)

sorus: Spore-producing area on the underside of a fern leaf.

spacing rod: A length of wood usually one inch by ten feet marked at one-foot intervals and used for spacing plants.

spading fork: A fork having several flat tines used for turning the soil. (9)

spadix: The thick, fleshy spike of flowers in the arum family, such as the "jack" in the jack-in-the-pulpit. (10)

spathe: The bract which surrounds a flower cluster. The "pulpit" or hood in the jack-in-the-pulpit. (10)

spawn: The mycelium of various fungi planted and from which mushrooms and toadstools develop. (11)

species: The fundamental unit of plant classification; the second name in the scientific binomial. (8)

specimen plant: A single plant grown as an ornamental in the landscape. (19)

sphagnum: A genus of mosses found in bogs where their debris is transformed into nearly sterile peat. (8)

spike: A simple inflorescence with flowers sessile on a single axis. (15)

spikelet: A unit of the inflorescence in grasses composed of two glumes and one or more florets. (16)

spiker: A roller with sharp spikes used to aerate sod or compacted ground. (9)

spike-toothed harrow: An implement with spike-like teeth dragged over the soil to break clods and level the field.

spindlebush: A system of training in which the tree is formed into a dwarf pyramid shape and the new shoots tied into a horizontal position. (13)

spine: A modified stem having a sharp point. (9)

spire: An obsolete term for a shoot. Also, to spindle, or become leggy. (10)

spit: A spade. Also, the depth of the blade of the spade; the cubical section of earth one spade wide, one deep, and one long. (11)

spitting: In hyacinths, the dropping of the whole flower during forcing. (9)

splice graft: A graft similar to the whip graft except that only a slanting cut, without the second tongue cut, is used.

split pit: The condition in stone fruit where the pit does not close completely. It is caused by abnormal fruit growth during the pit hardening stage. (9)

splitting: The malformation of a flower in carnation or poinsettias. (5)

spot board: (spotting board). A board having small dibbles attached in rows, used to make a preset number of planting holes in a flat of medium.

spot water: To apply water only to certain areas. (6)

spore: An asexual reproductive cell able to form a new plant. Common in the ferns and other lower plants. (8)

sport: (bud sport). A plant or plant part arising by spontaneous mutation. (4)

spreader: An implement for spreading fertilizer or other material. A compound added to a spray to enhance its spread over the surface of the foliage. A wooden or metal object used to spread young branches in a fruit tree. (9,17)

sprig: A small twig. A stolon or rhizome. (8)

sprigging: Propagation using stolons or rhizomes.

spring-toothed harrow: An implement with sharpened, curved blades of spring steel, dragged over the soil to break clods and smooth the field.

springwood: See earlywood.

sprout: The young growing shoot of a seed or bud. (8)

sprue: Poor, thin asparagus. (10)

spud: A long-handled chisel for cutting the taproots of certain weeds, such as dandelion. (11)

spur: A very short, stubby flowering branch with leaves and upon which fruit are borne, as in apple, pear, and plum. (9)

spur-type: A cultivar, usually of apple, that produces a greater number of spurs than normal. The tree is only 3/4 the height of a non spur-type on a similar rootstock.

square: An unopened cotton flower bud with accompanying bracts. (14)

St: See L. In corn, the disease resistance code for smut.

staddle: A fruit tree in which the trunk and primary scaffold system are developed from the rootstock and scions are topworked directly to the scaffolds. (13)

stage "G": The point of gynoecium formation in tulip and other members of the lily family. (9)

stamen: The male portion of the flower made up of the anther and the filament. (4)

staminate flower: A male flower. (4)

staminode: A rudimentary stamen.

stand: A group of plants growing together in one area, such as a stand of corn. (18)

standard: The inner, usually upright, three segments or petals of the iris flower. The top petal of the pea flower. Also, a treelike plant with the main stem unbranched. A tree not dwarfed by genetics or rootstock. (12)

starter fertilizer: A liquid or granular fertilizer applied in small amounts near the seed (granular) or in the planting hole (liquid) to accelerate the early growth of the plant. The dilute solution of a soluble fertilizer used on young plants to lessen transplant shock. (3,9)

stele: The vascular cylinder of a root.

stem: The stalk of a plant or plant part. More specifically, a shoot more than one year old. (8)

stem builder: See interstem.

stem topple: A physiological disorder in tulips causing the collapse of the stem just beneath the flower around the time of bloom. (9)

stick: (strike). To place unrooted cuttings in propagating media. (5)

sticker: A compound added to a pesticide to keep it from washing off the surface of the foliage. (9)

stigma: The tissue at the tip of the style which traps pollen and upon which it germinates. (4)

stipe: The stalk of a fern frond. Also, the stalk of a pistil. (10,15)

stipule: Small, leaflike appendage found near the base of some leaves. (4)

stock: (rootstock, understock). The root, or stem portion and root, upon which the scion is grafted. The shortened base of a stem. A tuberous, underground stem, as in the iris, used for food storage. (4,11)

stock plant: A plant used as a source of cuttings. (5)

stolon: (runner). A modified stem that grows along the soil surface and which may root or send out shoots at some of the nodes. (8)

stoloniferous: Bearing stolons. (4)

stoma: See stomate. pl. Stomata.

stomate: A very small opening in the surface of a leaf or young shoot for the exchange of gases and moisture. (4)

stone fruit: Fruit from plants of the genus *Prunus;* all having a hard pit. These include peach, apricot, nectarine, cherry, plum, and almond. (9)

stool: See layering. The base of a plant below ground level that gives rise to propagative organs, such as new shoots, for layering. Shoots that arise at this location and become rooted. Shoots that arise from below the soil line. (10,14)

stop: See pinch.

strain: A group within a cultivar with characteristics worthy of propagation but not of sufficient import to classify them as a different cultivar.

stratification: The exposure of moist seeds to cold temperatures to promote germination. (7)

strig: The stem by which the berry cluster is attached to the shoot in currants.

strike: See stick. Also, to emit roots, as from a cutting. (15)

strobile: A inflorescence with scales or bracts, as a pine cone. (15)

stubbing: See heading.

stubble culture: See no-till.

stumping: A form of mound layering.

style: A stalklike structure between the stigma and the ovary through which the pollen tube grows. (4)

style arm: The individually stigma-tipped division of a style. (12)

Su: See normal sugary.

suberized: Covered or impregnated with corky tissue. (4)

subshrub: A small shrub that is woody at its base only.

subsoil: Usually, that soil below plow layer (about eight inches). (1)

subsoiling: To loosen the subsoil without inversion and with a minimum of mixing of the subsoil with the surface soil. (3)

succession: The sequence in which plants follow each other. (8)

succession planting: (succession cropping). Planting one crop right after the harvest of another.

succulent: A plant with thick, juicy stems and leaves for conserving water. (8)

sucker: An adventitious shoot arising from the base of a plant or from the root. (4)

suffrutescent: Slightly woody. (15)

suffruticose: A perennial plant with the lower part of the stem or branches woody. (15)

sugary enhanced: (Se). A sweet corn cultivar having the gene responsible for production of tender kernels and the delayed conversion of sugar to starch after harvest. These cultivars require no isolation and produce ears sweeter than those with the normal sugary gene, but less sweet than the supersweet cultivars.

sugary enhanced +: (Se+, fully sugary enhanced). In sweet corn, the hybrids between two Se parents.

sulfate of ammonia: See ammonium sulfate.

sulfate of potash: See potassium sulfate.

sulfate of potash-magnesia: (Sul-Po-Mag). A fertilizer material containing at least 18% potassium, 11% magnesium sulfate, and at most, 2.5% chlorine. (1,2)

summer fallow: The tillage of noncropped land in summer to destroy weed growth and replenish soil moisture. (14)

summerwood: See latewood.

sunscald: Injury caused by thawing and then rapid freezing of a tree trunk exposed to strong sunlight or by extremes in winter temperatures. (9)

superior ovary: The development of the ovary above the other floral parts. A hypogenous flower.

superphosphate: See double superphosphate and normal superphosphate.

supersweet: (Sh_2). A sweet corn cultivar having the gene Sh_2 that allows the plant to produce twice the sugar of normal sweet corns and prevents that sugar from converting to starch after harvest. These cultivars must be isolated from other sweet corn.

surface soil: The top five to eight inches of the soil. (1)

surfactant: Material that lowers the surface tension of a liquid, improving the dispersal of a compound, usually a pesticide. (3,4)

suture: A line or seam joining the segments of some fruit. Also, the line on a peach, plum, cherry, and apricot.

Sw: In corn, the disease resistance code for Stewart's wilt.

swamp muck: See muck.

syncarp: A fleshy, aggregate fruit. (15)

synthetic manure: See compost.

syringe: To spray plants with water for the purpose of increasing the surrounding humidity or to remove pests and dust. (6)

systemic: Affecting the entire organism or, as in a pesticide, one that spreads through the entire vascular system of the plant. (4)

T

T: (TMV). In peppers and tomatoes, the disease resistance code for tobacco mosaic virus.

tamping: Firming loose soil with a flat surface, such as a board, spade, etc. (7)

tanglefoot: A sticky substance applied in a band around the trunk of a tree to prevent certain insects from climbing up to the foliage. (18)

tankage: The animal residue separated from fats and gelatin and dried. It contains about 7% nitrogen, 11% phosphorus, and 0.4% potash. Garbage tankage is the rendered, dried and ground residue remaining after the extraction of fat from discarded food products. It contains about 3% nitrogen, 3% phosphorus, and 1% potash. (1,2)

taproot: The main descending root of certain plants. (18)

tassel: The male flower in corn that appears at the top of the stalk.

taxonomy: The science dealing with the naming and classification of plants. (18)

temperature inversion: A situation where a lighter warm air mass is located above a heavier cold air mass, resulting in little air mixing and the accumulation of smog, dust, smoke, and frost. (8)

tendril: A long, thin, coiling structure on a stem that twists around a structure for support, as in peas and cucumbers. (4)

tension wood: Reaction wood in dicots formed on the upper sides of branches and crooked stems. (19)

tepal: A term for the combined petals and sepals of a flower, especially when they resemble each other, as in *Narcissus.*

terminal bud: A bud at the tip of a shoot.

terrace: A raised, level strip of ground usually constructed on a contour and supported on the downslope side by stones or other suitable material, designed to make the land tillable and less erodable. (3)

terrarium: A glass-enclosed case for growing plants. (18)

testa: The outer seed coat. (15)

TEV: In peppers, the disease resistance code for tobacco etch virus.

thatch: The buildup of a layer of dead and dying stems and leaves on the soil surface and below the green foliage of turf. (18)

thermodormancy: The high-temperature inhibition of seed germination. (17)

thigmotropism: The response of a plant or plant part to touch.

thimble pot: A small flower pot about two inches in diameter. (10)

thin: The removal of young plants from a row, excess shoots from a tree, excess buds from a shoot, or excess fruit from a tree.

thorn: A sharp, specialized shoot arising from the xylem. (8)

thrips: A small insect that damages plants.

thrum-eyed: A tubular flower wherein the stamens are visible but the stigmas are not. The opposite of pin-eyed. (10)

thumb pot: A small flower pot about 2.5 inches in diameter. (10)

tied-leaf: A condition in tulips wherein there is an unclear demarcation between the perianth and the last leaf. (9)

till: To prepare the soil for planting; to cultivate. (3)

tiller: A shoot arising from the base of a grass. (9)

tilth: A soil's physical condition related to its ease of tillage and fitness for a seedbed. (3)

tip: The removal of the tip portion of a shoot.

tipburn: The necrosis of the outer margins of the leaves caused by the environment or by a physiological disorder.

tissue culture: A method for rapid propagation of plants by growing callus tissue on agar plates in the laboratory.

TLS: In cucumbers, the disease resistance code for target leaf spot.

tobacco stems: The ground stems of the tobacco plant. They are sometimes used as a fertilizer containing about 2% nitrogen, 1% phosphorus, and 13% potash. (2)

tomato cage: A wire cone or cylinder used to support tomato plants. (19)

tongue graft: A graft wherein two slices are made in both the scion and the stock, the first downward on the scion and upward on the stock, the second in reverse, that is, upward on the scion and downward on the stock. The second cuts form tongues and should begin near the center of the pieces of wood. The tongues are then interlocked, providing a tightly fitting union.

top: To remove or heavily prune the top of a plant.

topdress: Fertilizer, compost, or other soil amendment spread over the top of plants to improve growth.

top-dressed fertilizer: Fertilizer applied to the soil after the crop becomes established.

topdressing: The application of fertilizer or topsoil to the soil's surface after plant establishment. (3)

topiary: The trimming and shaping of plants into the shapes of animals or geometric designs. It is usually done with evergreens. (8)

topsoil: The upper layer of rich soil, usually turned during normal cultivation. (3)

topwork: (top-graft). To graft over the top of a tree, usually with cleft-grafts. Done with fruit trees to change the cultivar.

trace element: See minor element.

training: Pruning and manipulating plants into a particular shape.

translocation: The movement of material and water from one part of the plant to another. (17)

transpiration: The loss of water from plant tissues, usually through the stomates. (4)

transplant: To move a plant from one place to another. (18)

treble superphosphate: See double superphosphate.

tree: A large woody plant usually with a single trunk. (8)

treillage: A trellis for vines or wires to which espaliers are fastened. (10)

trellis: An open frame or lattice used to support vines and other creeping plants. (8)

trench: To work manure or other organic matter and/or fertilizer into the top 18 inches of soil by double digging. (10)

tricalcium phosphate: See calcium phosphate.

trickle irrigation: See drip irrigation.

trifid: Divided into three parts. (16)

triple superphosphate: See double superphosphate.

tropism: The ability of a plant to be affected by some stimulus, such as light (phototropism), gravity (geotropism), touch (thigmotropism), and water (hydrotropism). (8)

trowel: A hand tool resembling a small spade used for planting seedlings, bulbs, etc. (9)

trumpet: The tubular corolla on flowers such as the *Narcissus.*

truss: A compact cluster of flowers at the end of a shoot, as in lilac. (10)

truncheon: Large branches removed from woody plants. (9)

tube: The narrow part of a corolla or calyx. (10)

tuber: An oval-shaped root or underground stem. Root tubers develop stems only at one end, while stem tubers can develop them along the entire axis. White potato is a stem tuber, dahlia and sweet potatoes are root tubers. (5,8)

tubercle: See nodule.

tuberous root: (root tuber). An enlarged, fleshy root, as in the sweet potato and dahlia. (14)

tulip dropper: A condition in tulips and occasionally in other bulb plants wherein a shoot grows down and produces a new bulb below the old one. (10)

tunic: Papery scales surrounding fleshy organs of bulbs or corms. (9)

tung meal: A meal derived from the ground seed of the tung tree. It contains about 4% nitrogen, 2% phosphorus, and 1% potash and is sometimes used as a fertilizer. (2)

turf: The mown sod of lawns.

turgid: Swollen due to the uptake of water. (4)

turgor: The normal inflation of cells due to internal pressure on the cell walls. (9)

turion: Adventitious shoot buds in certain plants, such as the raspberry. (9)

twig: A stem less than a year old. (19)

U

umbel: An inflorescence with the pedicels of the flowers arising from the same point. (15)

undersow: To broadcast cover crop seed a few weeks before a cash crop is to be harvested.

understock: See stock.

unisexual: A flower that bears either staminate or pistillate parts. (18)

unit: A unit of plant food is 1%, or 20 pounds per ton. (1)

unslaked lime: See lime.

urceolate: Urn-shaped. (15)

urea: A completely water-soluble material synthesized from ammonia and carbon dioxide and containing about 45% nitrogen. It also occurs naturally in urine, Peruvian guano, and poultry manure. As a fertilizer it can be applied to the soil or as a foliar spray directly to the plants. (1,2)

urea-formaldehyde: (urea-form). A combination of urea and formaldehyde used as a nitrogen fertilizer. The rate of its release of nitrogen is governed by the proportion of urea present; the more urea in the formula, the more quickly the nitrogen will become available for plant use. (1)

V

vanda: A type of orchid.

variegation: A mottled pattern of coloration of a leaf, flower, or other plant part because of nonuniform pigmentation. (4)

variety: A subdivision of a species. It is sometimes used interchangeably, but should not be confused, with "cultivar," which refers to a horticultural variety. (4)

vascular tissue: Conducting tissue for water and nutrients composed of the xylem, phloem, and cambium. (4)

vector: A carrier. Insects are often vectors for plant pathogens.

vegetative propagation: The production of new plants by means of nonsexual tissues. (18)

vein: A vascular bundle of a flower or leaf. (19)

velamin: The multiple layered epidermis of the root that absorbs water in epiphytic orchids. It also attaches the root to the host tree.

venation: The pattern of veins in a leaf. (11)

veneer graft: A type of side graft.

vermiculite: Magnesia mica heated to expand to many times its original volume. It absorbs large quantities of water and is used as a soil conditioner. (2)

vernalization: The condition whereby some plants require exposure to lower temperatures for an extended period in order to properly flower. (17)

vernation: The pattern of leaf arrangement in a bud. (11)

viable: The ability of a seed to remain alive and to produce a healthy seedling. (17)

vine: A plant, either herbaceous or woody, that climbs by means of tendrils, twining, or aerial rootlets. (8)

viticulture: The study of grape-growing. (4)

volunteer: A plant arising from natural seeding; not planted by humans.

W

warren-hoe: A heart shaped hoe used for opening a furrow. (11)

waterlogging: The complete replacement of soil air with water.

water plant: See aquatic.

water-slaked lime: See calcium oxide-hydrated.

water sprout: (watershoot). A vigorous shoot arising from the trunk or large branch that grows vertically and rapidly. (4)

water table: The upper surface of the ground water. If a hole is dug, water will fill the hole to the level of the water table.

weed: A plant growing out of place.

weeping: See bleeding. The drooping habit of branches in some species, such as "weeping cherry."

wet feet: A condition caused by excessive soil moisture.

wettable powder: A dry form of a chemical that will form a suspension when mixed with water.

wetting agent: A substance, such as soap, added to a spray solution that will allow for better contact, or wetting of the plant surface.

whip: A young, usually one year old, unbranched tree.

whip graft: A type of graft wherein the stock and scion are about the same diameter. Slanting cuts are first made in the ends of each and then a second, tongue cut is made in each and the tongues inserted into each other.

whorl: Three or more leaves, branches, or flowers arranged at the same point around the stem. (11)

wick watering: The practice wherein water moves from a container below to soil around the plant roots through a wick. (19)

wilding: (wildling). Wild, uncultivated plants, or plants escaped from cultivation. (10)

wilt: The condition wherein a plant droops because of a decrease in cell turgor due to lack of moisture or certain pathogens.

wilting coefficient: The point at which the water remaining in the soil is so tightly bound as to be unavailable to plants.

wilting point: The point of depletion of soil moisture when plants wilt. If they recover during the night or after watering, they are said to have undergone "incipient wilt." If they do not recover from a wilted condition, even after watering, they are said to have reached the "permanent wilting point."

windbreak: Trees, shrubs, or other structures set perpendicular to the principal wind direction to protect crops, soils, etc., from wind and snow drift. (3)

windburn: Scorching of foliage due to damaging winds. (10)

wing: A thin projection or border, such as on the rachis of some species of grass. (16)

winter annual: A hardy plant grown for its winter bloom in areas having a mild winter. (19)

witches'-broom: An abnormal growth of tufted, small, closely set branches found on a number of trees and shrubs, often caused by a virus or rust infection. (18)

WMV: In melons and cucumbers, the disease resistance code for watermelon mosaic virus. Numbers following the letters refer to the race of the pathogen.

wood ashes: A material having some fertilizer and liming value and containing about 2% phosphorus, 5% potassium, and 33% calcium. Wood ashes have a very high acidity-neutralizing potential. (2)

woody plant: A plant that produces woody stems and trunks that persist aboveground through the winter, from year to year, in zones where it is hardy. (18)

X

xerophyte: A plant adapted to arid conditions. (8)

xiphium: In irises, those of the Spanish or English type. (15)

xylem: The woody portion of a stem that conducts water and minerals and provides support. (4)

Y

yellows: A plant disease, usually caused by a virus, wherein the plant becomes yellow and stunted. (19)

Z

zinc sulfate: A water soluble zinc salt used to supply zinc to plants. (1)

zoning: The undesirable formation of alternating bands of light and dark tissue in the roots of beets.

zygomorphic flower: An irregularly shaped flower that is able to be divided into two halves along a single plane.

zygote: A fertilized egg.

ZYMV: In cucumbers, the disease resistance code for zucchini yellow mosaic virus.

Literature Cited

1. McVickar, M.H. and W.M. Walker. 1978. *Using Commercial Fertilizers.* The Interstate Publishers, Inc., Danville, IL, 61834. 363p.

2. Mehring, A.L. 1964. *Dictionary of Plant Foods.* Farm Chemicals. 56p.

3. *Glossary of Soil Science Terms.* 1987. Soil Science Society of America. 677 South Segoe Rd., Madison, WI, 53711. 44p.

4. Galletta, G.J. and D.G. Himelrick (eds.). 1990. *Small Fruit Crop Management.* Prentice Hall, Englewood Cliffs, NJ, 07632. 602p.

5. Nelson, K.S. 1991. *Flower and Plant Production in the Greenhouse.* 4th ed. Interstate Publishers, Inc., Danville, IL, 61834. 220p.

6. Nelson, K.S. 1966. *Flower and Plant Production in the Greenhouse.* Interstate Publishers, Inc., Danville, IL, 61834. 335p.

7. Bush-Brown, J. and L. Bush-Brown. 1965. *America's Garden Book.* Charles Scribner's Sons, NY. 752p.

8. Marsh, W.L. 1964. *Landscape Vocabulary.* Miramar Publishing Co., Los Angeles, CA. 316p.

9. Soule, J. 1985. *Glossary for Horticultural Crops.* John Wiley and Sons. NY. 898p.

10. Taylor, N. (ed.). 1938. *The Garden Dictionary.* Houghton Mifflin Co., Boston, MA. 888p.

11. Seymour, E.L.D. 1941. *The New Garden Encyclopedia.* W.H. Wise Co., NY. 1348p.

12. Anley, G. 1946. *Irises: Their Culture and Selection.* W.H. and L. Colling-ridge Ltd., London. 115p.

13. A Glossary of terms used in Pruning Fruit Trees. *Scientific Horticulture* 11:67-74.

14. Hartmann, H.T., A.M. Kofranek, V.E. Rubatsky, and W.J. Flocker. 1988. *Plant Science.* Prentice Hall, Englewood Cliffs, NJ, 07632. 674p.

15. Wymlan, D. 1977. *Wyman's Gardening Encyclopedia.* Macmillan Publishing Co., Inc., NY. 1221p.

16. Hitchcock, A.S. 1935. *Manual of the Grasses of the United States.* United States Department of Agriculture Misc. Pub. 200. 1040p.

17. Swiader, J.M., G.W. Ware, and J.P. McCollum. 1992. *Producing Vegetable Crops.* Interstate Publishers, Inc., Danville, IL, 61834. 626p.

18. Hull, G.F. 1967. *The Language of Gardening: An Informal Dictionary.* The World Publishing Co., NY. 191p.

19. Klein, R.M. and D.T. Klein. 1988. *Fundamentals of Plant Science.* Harper and Row, NY. 617p.